BONSAI

The Complete Step-by-Step Guide on How to Cultivate and Care for Beginners

By Kitaro Takagi

© **Copyright 2021 - All rights reserved.**

The content contained within this book may not be reproduced, duplicated or transmitted without direct written permission from the author or the publisher.

Under no circumstances will any blame or legal responsibility be held against the publisher, or author, for any damages, reparation, or monetary loss due to the information contained within this book. Either directly or indirectly.

Legal Notice:

This book is copyright protected. This book is only for personal use. You cannot amend, distribute, sell, use, quote or paraphrase any part, or the content within this book, without the consent of the author or publisher.

Disclaimer Notice:

Please note the information contained within this document is for educational and entertainment purposes only. All effort has been executed to present accurate, up to date, and reliable, complete information. No warranties of any kind are declared or implied. Readers acknowledge that the author is not engaging in the rendering of legal, financial, medical or professional advice. The content within this book has been derived from various sources. Please consult a licensed professional before attempting any techniques outlined in this book.

By reading this document, the reader agrees that under no

BONSAI

circumstances is the author responsible for any losses, direct or indirect, which are incurred as a result of the use of information contained within this document, including, but not limited to, — errors, omissions, or inaccuracies.

BONSAI

Table of Contents

Introduction xii

Chapter One: Why Bonsai? The History and Benefits of the Art of Growing Miniature Trees 1

   What is Bonsai? 2

   What Makes a Bonsai a Bonsai? 4

   Why Should I Create a Bonsai? 5

   It Reminds You to Slow Down 5

   It Introduces Spiritual Energy to Your Home 6

   It's a Constant Form of Art 7

   It Doesn't Require a Yard 7

   It Creates Natural Beauty 7

   It's a Lifetime Connection between Generations 8

   It Creates an Emotional Commitment 8

   The Origins of Bonsai 9

   Benefits of Caring for a Bonsai Tree 11

   Stress Relief 11

   Physical Activity 11

   Patience 12

   Purifying the Air 12

Chapter Two: Bonsai Aesthetics 14

   Leaf Reduction 16

   Miniaturization 17

   Ramification 18

   Gravitas 18

BONSAI

Lignification 18

Curvature 18

Nebari 19

Deadwood 19

General Guidelines 19

Chapter Three: The Necessary Tools 22

Tweezers 24

Wire Pliers 24

Pruning Shears 25

Branch Cutters 25

Knob Cutters 26

Concave Cutters 26

Root Hook 27

Root Rake 27

Root Cutters 27

Wire Cutters 28

Wound Sealers 28

Training Wire 29

Bending Clamps 30

Chapter Four: Types of Bonsai 32

Cedar 33

Caring for Your Bonsai 34

Dwarf Jade 36

Caring for Your Bonsai 37

Ficus 38

Caring for Your Bonsai 39

Japanese Maple 41

Caring for Your Bonsai 42

Japanese Flowering Cherry 44

Caring for Your Bonsai 45

Juniper 46

Caring for Your Bonsai 47

Pine 50

Caring for Your Bonsai 51

Pomegranate 54

Caring for Your Bonsai 55

Other Favorite Bonsai Species 57

Apple trees 57

Azalea trees 57

Bamboo 57

Money tree 58

Honeysuckle 58

Chapter Five: Bonsai Styles 60

Formal Upright (Chokkan) 61

Recommended Species 62

Recommended Containers 62

Informal Upright (Moyogi) 63

Recommended Species 63

Recommended Containers 63

Slanting (Shakan) 63

Recommended Species *64*

Recommended Containers *64*

Cascade (Kengai) 64

Recommended Species *65*

Recommended Containers *65*

Semi-Cascade (Han-Kengai) 65

Recommended Species *66*

Recommended Containers *66*

Windswept (Fukinagashi) 66

Recommended Species *67*

Recommended Containers *67*

Literati (Bunjin) 67

Recommended Species *67*

Recommended Containers *68*

Chapter Six: Choosing Your Bonsai Tree 70

Where Will Your Tree Grow? 71

Size of Your Desired Tree 72

Style Chosen for Your Bonsai 72

Your Skill Level 73

How to Choose the Right Tree 73

Starter Trees, Cuttings, and Seeds 74

Checking the Health 75

Chapter Seven: Cultivating Your Bonsai 77

Soil 78

Soil Requirements 79

What Is Soil Made From? 80

Making Your Own Bonsai Soil 81

Choosing the Deep Enough Container 82

Fertilizing 83

The Purpose of Fertilization 83

NPK Numbers 84

> *Nitrogen* 85
>
> *Phosphorus* 85
>
> *Potassium* 85

When to Fertilize 85

> *Deciduous Trees* 85
>
> *Conifer Bonsai Trees* 86
>
> *Tropical or Subtropical Trees* 86

Liquid vs. Slow-Release Fertilizers 86

How to Fertilize Your Tree 87

What Makes a Good Fertilizer? 87

Watering 88

How Often You Should Water Your Bonsai 88

How to Water Your Bonsai 89

Should You Water All of Your Bonsai at the 90

When Should You Water? 90

What Kind of Water? 90

Misting Your Plant 91

What About Vacations? 91

Lighting 92

Fluorescent Lights 92

HID Lights... 93

LED Lights 93

Lighting for Your Bonsai.. 94

Propagation... 95

Growing from Seed 95

Growing From Cuttings 97

Chapter Eight: Pruning and Trimming Your Bonsai 102

Masculine vs. Feminine.. 103

Pruning Your Bonsai.. 104

Why Bonsais Need Pruning 105

Structural Pruning....................................... 105

Maintenance Pruning................................... 106

How to Prune Your Bonsai Tree 107

After Pruning Care... 109

Chapter Nine: Wiring Your Bonsai 111

Benefits of Bonsai Wiring................................... 112

Choosing Wire.. 113

When to Wire 114

How to Wire 115

Removing the Wire.. 116

Chapter Ten: Repotting 118

What is Repotting?... 119

Why Repot the Bonsai?....................................... 120

When to Repot 121

Root Pruning 122

How to Repot 123

Chapter Eleven: Seasonal Care 127

Fall Care 128

Enough Sunlight for the Trees 129

Adjust the Watering Schedule 130

Fertilize 130

Double-Check the Drainage of your Tree's Pot 130

Final Pruning and Wiring for the Year 131

Winter Care 132

Dormancy and Your Bonsai 133

Preparing for the Winter 134

During Winter Care 135

After Winter Care 135

What About Tropical and Subtropical Bonsais? 135

Chapter Twelve: Showing Off Your Bonsai 138

The Basics of Bonsai Display 139

The Bonsai is the Center 139

Bonsai Displays Create Harmony 140

Everything Should Be Intentional 140

The Elements of a Bonsai Display 140

Companion Objects 141

Pot 142

The Stand 142

Placing the Display 143

Placing the Bonsai 143

Placing the Companion Objects 144

Choosing the Perfect Container 144

Masculine vs. Feminine Pots 145

Pot Shape 146

Pot Rim 146

Pot Feet 146

Pot Corners 147

Pot Colors 147

Pot Textures 149

Final Words 152

INTRODUCTION

If you've ever seen a well-maintained bonsai in all its glory, you've seen the beauty, grace, and majestic air of a large tree that's been condensed down to something small enough to put on a shelf. It is something that is beautiful to behold, and everyone should see it at least once in their lives. If you're particularly ambitious, you might even make it a point to try to grow your own tree.

BONSAI

Bonsais are beautiful; there is no doubt about it. However, what most people tend to forget is that with such beauty comes a lot of maintenance. It's not as simple as lopping off a bunch of branches until the tree stays the size you want. It takes a great deal of care to create those beautiful, fantastic designs that are so appealing. Even then, you have to have a tree that will transform into the bonsai you want, and that can take plenty of time.

Being able to take a sapling and transform it into a bonsai may be time-consuming, but it is absolutely worth the effort if you've got the time and drive for it. Nurturing something into a beautiful piece of art can be incredibly satisfying. You can use several different methods to create the bonsai of your dreams, and as you read this book, you'll discover several of the methods that will aid that process.

You will not get the bonsai of your dreams overnight, but remember that every time you prune your tree, attach the wiring, and train your plant to grow, you are helping to create the end product. Every action over the years you train your bonsai will help create something beautiful that you can cherish, knowing that it was your tender love and care that grew it.

Bonsais can make perfect conversation pieces, and they show your patience and dedication to something other than yourself. Cultivating your own bonsai is difficult due to the sheer time commitment. Many people prefer to purchase bonsais that are already ready to care for, but you can also grow your own from seed and spend several years training it. Or you can purchase small saplings to find one that will perfectly fit your vision.

The whimsy captured by the bonsai is almost unparalleled. They look as if they're right out of a fantasy storybook, with the thick trunk, outstretched limbs, and miniature foliage that grows across it. The trunk is reminiscent of the look of a fully mature tree instead of looking narrow and weak, like most younger trees. The leaves are like miniature versions of the ones on an adult tree, and they may even flower, depending upon the tree.

If you're ready to start understanding how to cultivate and care for your own bonsai, you're in the right spot. We're going to discuss all of the pertinent details, from what makes a bonsai a bonsai to the various styles that are used to create the typical look associated with them. We'll discuss the various types of trees that are commonly used to create the bonsai look and how to choose out the perfect tree. We will also take time to discuss cultivating, trimming, pruning, wiring, and caring for trees to ensure that you're well-prepared to meet any of your tree's needs.

At the end of this long, tedious process of caring for your tree, you will have your own little piece of art that you can enjoy and show off. People will marvel at how great it will look, and you'll be able to tell them that you put in so much work to create the look. So, what are you waiting for? It's time to get started and learn.

CHAPTER ONE

WHY BONSAI?

THE HISTORY AND BENEFITS OF THE ART OF GROWING MINIATURE TREES

Bonsai trees are beautiful. They are small but still manage to have the majesty that you'd expect of a fully grown tree. If you're unsure whether you want to grow your own bonsai, being informed is a good starting point to recognize what you need to do. We'll begin with defining a bonsai and understanding what separates a bonsai from a dwarf tree. They're not exactly the same thing. We'll go over why you should consider creating your own bonsai so you can start weighing whether this is the right hobby for you to pick. It isn't right for everyone.

What is Bonsai?

You probably have a pretty clear idea in your mind about what a bonsai tree is. It's one of those little trees in a little flat pot with a stunted trunk and bushy leaves that have been shaped into perfection, right? Well… Technically. However, there is more to it than that, and bonsai trees have an appeal that attracts people around the world into trying out the hobby. Initially originating in China, the meticulous process of grooming trees into perfection spread across the world. Many people can

BONSAI

recognize a bonsai tree at first glance, especially if it were a beautiful Japanese maple with brilliant red foliage.

The word as we know it is Japanese for "Planted in a container." The Japanese have taken the Chinese art of miniaturizing trees and began honing that art into what we know it to be today—carefully sculpted trees that are more refined and have undergone more grooming and trimming to create the look we tend to recognize. Chinese trees are typically much truer to the ancient art and may appear to be almost crude in comparison. However, this is just because of different influences and preferences.

Bonsai is used to describe any shrub or tree that has been meticulously miniaturized through several different processes, primarily pruning and tying branches to influence them. There are no one specific species that must be used, and bonsai can refer to any tree that has been molded appropriately. However, keep in mind that it is a form of art that is meant to reflect nature. It's designed to pay homage to the world and its interconnectedness. It is to honor the beauty that can be found in nature at a glance. The trees are shaped in different manners to convey different meanings as well. They are personal vessels for expression that can be used to carefully craft something into a new form.

There is a major difference that must first be noted before we continue. We commonly hear about dwarf trees that grow to significantly smaller proportions than others of their variety. However, these aren't the same as bonsai trees. Bonsai is a miniature-sized tree that is trimmed from a regular tree. Dwarf trees, however, will only grow to a shorter size. This is done through selective breeding and stunting processes to prevent the trees from growing to their usual sizes.

A bonsai tree without any further grooming and planted in an appropriate natural habitat will grow to normal size. A dwarf tree never will. You aren't changing the DNA or the nature of the tree; you're only changing the way that it grows by manipulating and trimming it to do what you want.

What Makes a Bonsai a Bonsai?

A bonsai is supposed to be a replica of what can be seen in nature. It is supposed to appear natural and unchanged by people, despite the manipulation that you'll make. There isn't one specific tree that must be transformed; there isn't even just one type of pattern that is necessary to create the bonsai look. There are several different options you can consider, depending upon who is doing the cultivating and what that person wants. So long as it is a plant in a container that has been shaped with bonsai strategies, it will be deemed a bonsai.

Keep in mind that there is no such thing as a finished bonsai. As long as the tree continues to grow, it will need constant care, or it will grow larger. It is a daily responsibility, but this is something that many bonsai gardeners love about the art. It is timeless and continues indefinitely. The constant effort that goes into caring for them makes the art that much more impressive.

BONSAI

Why Should I Create a Bonsai?

If you're still on the fence about creating your own bonsai, you're probably wondering what could convince you to make a decision. It is an immensely personal decision to make a bonsai tree grow, so only you can know if it is right for you. Are you willing to put in constant effort to keep your tree healthy? Some people love the ritualistic care that their trees need to continue the hobby. Others find that they'd rather just get an artificial tree to enjoy the look without the effort at all. What you choose to do is up to you. However, if you're on the fence, consider some of these reasons that you may want to create a bonsai.

It Reminds You to Slow Down

Most people are too busy getting caught up with running around. They're constantly juggling so many different things: jobs, relationships, and chores. It's hard to find time for anything else. However, with bonsai, you teach yourself to slow down. You're mindfully connecting with your tree. So many of the modern urban environments are full of attempts to simplify the process, such as taking plants that have already been mostly grown and simply planting them in your garden instead of taking the time to carefully cultivate the garden.

Implementing care for a bonsai in your routine means you have to slow down. You need to settle into the more unhurried pace to take care of the plant. You're going to be reminded of the importance of patience as you watch your plant thrive. Nothing will help your plant grow quicker than it already is doing. However, as you force yourself to slow down, you get to enjoy those moments of quiet solitude and appreciation where you can see the perseverance of nature as the tree continues to grow while you care for it. It is a process that involves both the tree and the person in unison working to create the result. As you tend to the tree, the tree will respond to what you want it to do.

It Introduces Spiritual Energy to Your Home

If you're looking for something to bring balance and spiritual energy into your home or space of your choice, bonsai is a perfect way to get started. With bonsai, you'll be creating a natural balance between the two. Successfully creating a bonsai means you are trying to balance the tree's propensity to grow and your own actions as you influence the nature around you.

As you create your bonsai, you bring both wood and earth, two important elements in feng shui, which is influential to bonsai, into your home. These create a positive flow of energy that should help your home.

It's a Constant Form of Art

If you love art but hate having to come up with new projects every time you finish the last one, and you're struggling with any sort of inspiration, you've got the constant influence of bonsai trees to your advantage. If you want to continue to have a beautiful tree that you have transformed into a bonsai masterpiece, you have to continue to work on it. This can be a great way to maintain some sort of constant force in your daily schedule. If you suffer from anxiety, you may find that the predictability of creating a bonsai helps you immensely.

It Doesn't Require a Yard

Because gardening often requires you to have some sort of access to the outdoors, it can be somewhat difficult for people who live in urban environments to find chances to do any gardening. However, with a bonsai tree, you don't have to worry so much about space. You can bring a tree inside to enjoy in your home, on a balcony, or moving back and forth between the two. Because you're able to grow a tree in your home, you then get the added benefit of being able to enjoy a tree inside, which can be uplifting when you're stressed.

It Creates Natural Beauty

As you create your bonsai, you are collaborating between yourself and the tree that you are trying to grow. What this means for you is that you are constantly making changes to which the tree responds. You bring your vision and essence, and the tree brings its own essence. Together, you get a one-of-a-kind bonsai tree. There will never be another one that looks like the tree that you've grown. It is perfectly unique—an amalgamation of your innermost self, thoughts, and the tree that you're growing.

It's a Lifetime Connection between Generations

If you're really dedicated to your bonsai, you may make a point of raising your tree and passing it down your family line. Some trees are capable of surviving for far longer than we'd expect. In some cases, they are able to thrive and grow for hundreds of years. As you grow a bonsai, you can pass it on to another family member as a memorial. It can become an heirloom, and as you bequeath it, you give all of the love and care that you've put into your tree to someone else to cultivate and love.

It Creates an Emotional Commitment

You are bound to get attached to your bonsai as you grow and nurture it. You're going to feel like you are much more connected to it and, therefore, you're much more likely to feel an emotional bond. This is because you've spent time and effort nurturing it. You've come to know it inside and out, recognizing what it likes and needs while also acknowledging what doesn't work for it. The connections you'll foster will last a lifetime, and often, people feel a deep attachment for the ones they grow, similar to how they'd feel about a pet.

BONSAI

The Origins of Bonsai

Despite the typical association with Japan, China served as the origin of bonsai. From there, it was able to spread to Korea before finally reaching Japan, brought by Buddhist monks who wanted to have access to nature within their temples. Manuscripts and paintings show that bonsais go back at least as far as 600 AD, but it's believed that potted trees were likely linked as far back as even 1000 BC.

The trees were based upon the miniature trees known to grow in the higher areas of mountains, where conditions were so harsh that the trees struggled to reach their typical full growth. However, they were still able to grow, albeit small and almost gnarled in their appearance. They became highly sought after and mimicked, giving birth to Penjing, the art of displaying mini landscapes on top of earthenware.

In order to mimic the knotted and gnarled look that the trees in the mountains had developed, early cultivators started pruning and binding the trees to create the twisted look and the aged appearances. It is possible they were designed to look like Chinese dragons and serpents or to mimic yoga positions.

It wasn't until the 12th century that bonsai trees were introduced to Japan and created what we know today. However, before the bonsai made it to Japan, the Chinese were cultivating their plants artistically on miniature scales to create a sort of balance to their own landscapes. The

BONSAI

Chinese grew to love the idea of miniaturizing their plants and focused on mastering the art. To them, the miniature objects were mystical and powerful.

As these early growers continued to develop their trees and the arts they used to keep them small, they also worked on creating ceramic containers that would catch the eye. The container was just as important as the plant itself. These early growers created beautiful ceramic designs and containers that are, to this day, coveted for Japanese bonsai as well.

As monks migrated from China to Japan and other parts of Asia, bringing with them their miniature trees, they began teaching others about the art. Various areas chose their own ways to create the craft and took their own liberties to grow them according to their desires. And thus, penzai, or Penjing, became Japanese bonsai.

The Japanese trees were around two feet tall, requiring years and years of care to carefully coax branches into position with bamboo and wire. New branches would even sometimes be grafted to the trees. They became royal status symbols.

By the 1600s, Japanese bonsai continued to grow and change. Artists began creating a minimalistic approach to bonsai, removing everything that was not essential to the plants. This was meant to mimic the Japanese philosophy of minimalism for a happier life.

BONSAI

Nowadays, people around the world seek to create beautiful trees that are able to grow indoors and out, creating gorgeous miniaturized landscapes to enjoy. No matter the social status of the individual, bonsai creates a welcome addition to just about any household.

Benefits of Caring for a Bonsai Tree

If you want to get your hands on a bonsai tree, you have a few different options. However, before we do this, let's consider some of the benefits that you'll gain. By gardening, you're already taking a more active, mindful approach to life and the world around you. You're creating a skill that is likely to keep you engaged and at peace. Gently caring for your bonsai may become part of your calming-down ritual each night. And if not, it could be. Did you know that gardening is good for your mental health? Bonsai is no exception to this.

Stress Relief

Taking care of your bonsai becomes a way to calmly keep yourself focused. If you're too rough, you could damage delicate twigs and branches that would take months or years to grow back. You could accidentally make a wrong cut as you trim your plant. It's relaxing to get into the groove and take care of your garden, and the more you do it, the better you'll feel.

Physical Activity

There is a physical activity aspect to gardening as well. While you may not be down on your knees pulling weeds, you're still likely to be on your feet, moving around, and carrying your garden around. You're likely to work hard on trimming, fertilizing, and otherwise caring for your garden.

Patience

With how much care you have to give your bonsai, you're naturally likely to build up the patience needed to deal with the endless watering, pruning, and caring required. The more you work on your tree, the better it will look and the nicer it will become. You'll also learn that patience is truly a virtue and that you should be patient more often.

Purifying the Air

Bonsais, like all plants, purify the air around them. They take in carbon dioxide and leave you with fresh, clean air. While a bonsai tree may only absorb a small amount of carbon dioxide, it is still something that you can use to freshen things up a little bit.

BONSAI

Chapter Summary

In this chapter, we have explored the history of bonsai cultivation and the reasons for engaging in this artistic hobby. Specifically, we've discussed the following topics:

- The Chinese origins of bonsai;
- The spread of the art form to Japan;
- The spread of bonsai cultivation outside of Japan;
- The modern tradition of bonsai cultivation;
- The scientific benefits of cultivating bonsai;
- The spiritual benefits of cultivating bonsai.

In the next chapter, you will learn about the different bonsai aesthetics.

CHAPTER TWO

BONSAI AESTHETICS

BONSAI

Bonsai trees have undoubted aesthetics. While no two trees look exactly the same, there are still several distinctive qualities that bonsais possess. These aesthetics serve as goals and characteristics that you'd like to see in your plant as you grow. They emphasize the Japanese traditions that are used to create beautiful trees with a wide range of aesthetics.

Just like all artists have their personal taste, bonsai trees come in all shapes and forms that are as unique as the people behind them. The goal is to create beautiful trees, but what is it that makes something beautiful? it depends on the person. Standards of beauty can change dramatically.

The shapes that you see in bonsai plants vary greatly, but they have similar themes. The tree should appear as natural as possible from the front. People viewing the tree from the front should not be able to spot any of the wiring or framing that goes into creating the tree. From the back, they should also be clean and organized as much as possible.

Because growing a bonsai isn't the same as being able to grow any old garden plant, it's important for people to recognize that many different flourishes may be introduced as well. This is where many of these aesthetics come in; they're artistic representations of the ideals of beauty. You are not only planting your shrub; you are creating the flourishes that you want to sculpt your tree into a sort of living testament of your mindset.

Bonsai trees are meant to have a solid visual balance—either static or dynamic. Static trees are meant to appear almost restful in appearance, upright, and usually quite symmetrical to create good, solid balance. Dynamic trees are asymmetrical to try to create instability and movement, such as wind blowing through the tree.

The trunks, branches, foliage, roots, and other parts of the tree are all manipulated with several aesthetic techniques. These are meant to create proportion and balance that can be used to ensure that the tree looks good. However, no matter the elements used, it is important to maintain a proportion similar to that of a fully grown tree. The foliage should be proportionate to the trees themselves, with the only real exception being for fruiting and flowering trees.

However, in art, rules are meant to be broken. While we'll be going over the traditional rules and aspects of bonsai, don't feel like you have to hold yourself back if you have a set vision in mind. If you do, you can still follow it. Unless you're competing for a perfect bonsai tree in a competition, no one is going to care if your proportions are a little bit off because you have a set vision. Art is all about flexibility and fluidity of expectations.

Leaf Reduction

We commonly refer to leaf reduction as pruning. This is meant to eliminate too many leaves from growing on the tree. Too many leaves cause a cluttered appearance to a tree that wouldn't allow you to enjoy the individual leaves

BONSAI

and design that is desired. Therefore, it is important to remove leaves that are unnecessary. This method has been used for centuries to help trim and regulate plants.

In order to effectively remove leaves, the tree may need to go through several periods of reduction, especially before any desired exhibitions. Pruning may also include total defoliation if necessary. Typically, it's easier to reduce leaves than it is to reduce needles.

Miniaturization

Miniaturization refers to the process by which the tree is kept small enough to grow in a container. The tree is supposed to look like a miniature replica of the tree in a state of nature, contained in a smaller container or pot. The key here is that you want the look of maturity without the size. Bonsai trees are expected to be small enough to maintain a mature appearance in a container. They're typically described by sizes.

- Mame refers to those less than 4 inches. They can be held in the palm of the hand.

- Shohin trees are 10 inches tall.

- All others are typically too large to move.

Smaller trees can't be altered as much as larger ones due to their small stature and the difficulty of shaping.

Ramification

Ramification is the process of splitting twigs to prevent unwanted branches and stems. Typically, this is used alongside leaf reduction, creating more consistent results of lessened leaves.

Gravitas

Gravitas refers to the maturity a tree commands. It is the ability of the plant to command attention and the air of maturity without growing any larger. It is supposed to create a balanced look that can be enjoyed by all. Effectively, it demonstrates the idea of physical weight that isn't actually there.

Lignification

Lignification is an enhancement of the woody look that a bonsai's trunk or branches may take. It is meant to look like mature bark, rough and dark in color. It should be designed to mimic the look of mature wood for whatever your particular species of tree would have in nature.

Curvature

Curvature isn't necessary but can allow for a perception of sturdiness and maturity. The tree's branches and trunk may be curved or contorted to shape the tree. Typically, branches may be curved so they aren't crossing or running into each other. To curve the trunk between the lowest branch and the roots is called *tachiagari*.

BONSAI

Nebari

In English, this is referred to as "buttressing." It is the spread that roots take above ground at the base of bonsai trees. If you've ever looked at the base of a mature tree, you know that you can see the roots start to spread out just above the ground. This is an important aspect of bonsai as it allows you to create a more mature-looking tree. You need well-set roots in order to have a plant that grows well, so you'll need to emphasize this.

Deadwood

When you grow a bonsai tree, you may want it to look a bit more mature and realistic, so you use deadwood to achieve the look. The deadwood can remain in place for years. Sometimes, trees may have branches snapped, and others may have a split trunk look. There are many different ways to implement deadwood looks, depending upon the effect you're looking to achieve.

General Guidelines

If you decide to keep your bonsai tree compliant with standards for yourself, you'll need to follow specific guidelines that will help determine that. Some of the most common guidelines include:

- The tree is in a small, formal container
- The only other living vegetation in your container is moss, which is optional.

BONSAI

- Nothing but rocks (optional), soil, and moss should appear beside your bonsai in the pot

- The tree should have a front and back.

- The tree should be tapered from the bottom to the top

- Roots should be exposed around the base and spread out as the tree enters the soil

- The tree should not have any visible root crossing

- Branches shouldn't appear before the first third of the trunk, at which point they should continue to the tip

- Branches should become smaller as they move up toward the top of the tree

- No major branches should cross in the front

- Ramification should increase toward the tips of branches

- Branch shape should appear heavy and dip downward

- The trunk may be straight or contorted but should lean slightly toward the viewer

- Foliage should be proportionate with the tree

BONSAI

Chapter Summary

In this chapter, we have explored bonsai aesthetics. Specifically, we've discussed the following topics:

- The general bonsai aesthetic principles;
- The aesthetic guidelines to help you achieve those principles;

In the next chapter, you will learn about the different bonsai styles.

BONSAI

CHAPTER THREE

THE NECESSARY TOOLS

If you want to enjoy a beautiful bonsai, it's not as simple as using a pair of kitchen scissors to chop off

BONSAI

branches and hope that everything ends up okay. You'll need to have several tools you can use to ensure that everything goes into place properly. New bonsai users usually think they don't need many things, but there are several tools that you're going to want to have in your arsenal.

Your bonsai is a reflection upon your internal self, brought out onto the tree that you've chosen to cultivate. With these tools at your disposal, you should find that the process gets a lot easier. Whether you want a conifer or deciduous tree, and no matter what the size, you're going to be able to bring your vision to life.

Before you purchase any tools, make sure you do your research. Ensure that the brand you've selected is trustworthy. Research them well and check out the reviews. You want to choose tools that are both high-quality and consistent in the quality they deliver. They should also be comfortable in your hands, so you find the entire process enjoyable.

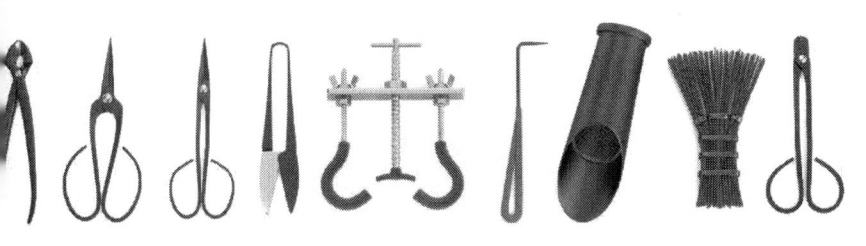

Tweezers

Angled tweezers are one of the cheapest tools you can get, but cheap doesn't mean you should skimp on the quality. Having a good pair of tweezers is one of the most important tools you can have. A good pair of tweezers allow you to access areas where you want to have the most control, while a bad pair is simply going to be frustrating to use.

When you have to remove weeds, hold parts of the tree out of the way, or generally clean out the space you're growing in, you need to have a good pair of tweezers. Make sure the tips aren't too narrow. Otherwise, instead of being able to pluck out weeds, you're going to slice right through them instead.

Along with the angled pair, you need a straight pair of tweezers if you intend to pull leaves or needles. These work by letting you pluck what you need to remove instead of having the angled elbow pinching at other foliage that you aren't trying to pull.

Thankfully, tweezers are easy to get your hands on. You don't have to find a pair that is specific to bonsai. Any pairs that have the angled and straight tips will work, so long as they're the right size. You don't want them to open much more than ¼" inch; otherwise, you're constantly applying pressure so you can navigate through your tree's foliage. This will quickly wear out your fingers.

Wire Pliers

BONSAI

Pruning Shears

Pruning shears are essential to managing your bonsai's foliage. The tips are narrow enough to navigate through branches, so you'll be able to get much cleaner and more precise cuts as you shape the branches. They should be comfortable and should cut cleanly in order to be effective. Make sure you choose a good pair rather than trying to substitute a pair of scissors.

Pruning Saws

Sometimes, you want to use a pruning saw to cut through branches manually. Using a pruning saw is the perfect way to do so. Typically, they're designed to cut when you pull to keep a smooth, clean cut.

Branch Cutters

Cutting deep into thick branches at the very surface of the trunk is difficult with a pair of run-of-the-mill scissors. If you want a clean, close cut that minimizes damage to the tree, you'll need to use branch cutters. These tools will help you avoid having a raised area as a result of branches being removed. While you might think that the little area left behind after branch removal is no big deal, the truth is, the more it heals, the worse it looks. It will grow more pronounced and become more obvious, which can be a problem if it's in the front of your tree. This is where ensuring a close cut comes into play; it will help to hide the mark.

Your branch cutter's blade should be roughly a third of the length of a branch you choose to cut. This means that you're going to need several pairs of cutters in different sizes, so you don't unintentionally break the cutters while leaving behind a damaged branch. You may also want some pairs that are thinner and meant to get into narrow areas that may otherwise be difficult to access.

Knob Cutters

Sometimes, you want to shape your tree without knobs left behind. This is where knob cutters come into play. A pair of knob cutters are shaped in a way that allows the blades to cut into the trunk, creating a slight indentation instead of leaving a knob behind. This allows for the tree to have a better, more managed look while also granting you the benefit of being able to reduce the healing time of your tree.

The blades that come together to make the cut are essentially cut like halves of spheres, which allows it to take the bite into the wood. This allows for the quick removal of more wood without sacrificing precision.

Concave Cutters

Concave branch cutters work as a sort of hybrid between the knob and branch cutters. They're designed as an easy 2-in-1 tool that will allow for functionality with a single tool. Typically, higher-quality concave cutters will be more expensive, but that's because it is difficult to produce a cutter that is just right. This is because when you're cutting into branches, you must be careful that you are not damaging anything in the process.

Root Hook

When it's time to transplant your tree, you'll need a root hook. This tool is designed to loosen the soil while also combing out your roots so you can ensure they're nice and neat before replanting them. It also serves as a great tool to aerate compact soil. Typically, these tools are somewhat small, but that allows for the precision necessary to work with the exact location of your root structure while working on repotting. You'll need certainty in the process, recognizing where the delicate root system is. If you're not careful, the roots you're trying to move around could become damaged beyond repair and kill your tree.

Root Rake

If you need to remove soil from around your tree's roots so you can aerate or weed it, you'll want to have a way to rake through the roots. Raking through the roots frees up soil and aerates it before you repot.

Root Cutters

When you repot your bonsai, you may need to work the roots to ensure they fit appropriately. This means having a tool that will be sufficient for the job. Some people may choose to substitute scissors here, but nothing can beat the ease of using root cutters. You'll be able to get in all the right angles to trim and groom your roots to perfection. Beyond that, you can also use these tools to reduce branch stubs as well.

Wire Cutters

You might think that any old wire cutters from the hardware store will be right for you, but these are often not quite right. Regular wire cutters can cause damage to your tree with their sharp tips being able to gouge into the delicate branches or the tree trunk. Instead of using any old pair, find a pair designed for bonsai. Typically, these have a round head with jaws that will allow you to cut the wire easily. While the price for wire cutters may seem to be intimidating, this is one of the tools that you should not negotiate on.

You might be tempted just to use your shears to cut through wire, but you can damage them. When you need to cut wire, you're trying to squeeze the metal in two. On the other hand, you can slice through branches relatively easily with the right tools. If you damage the shears, you can make it more difficult for them to cut cleanly through any branches that you choose to remove.

Wound Sealers

Remember, when you trim your bonsai tree to shape it, you're probably going to remove at least a few major branches that are going to be visible. Typically, scars should not be visible from the front at all, and you'll need wound sealers to help during this process.

BONSAI

When you cut into your tree, it doesn't heal from the inside out. Rather, it creates callus tissue that goes over the wound. This keeps it from allowing any dangerous pathogens inside but can also be quite ugly to view. The callus tissue is essentially like a scar on yourself. Wound sealers can help to protect your tree before the callus forms.

When you purchase a wound sealer, you speed up the healing process. Conifers, in particular, are notorious for taking much longer to heal than other types of trees, so being able to seal any wounds could be the difference between your tree surviving well or getting sick in the process of healing.

Training Wire

When you want to shape your tree, you'll need wire to do so. Typically, training wire is used to guide your tree to the positions that you want it to be in. Leave the wire in place long enough to train the trunk and branches to get them in the right spots. It's a temporary device that helps move things along and is then removed when done. The wire can bend branches and trunks, typically because it's the quickest way to shape them, though there are other options as well. You don't necessarily *have* to use wire to shape the trees, but many people tend to turn to it.

You can typically use any kind of wire to shape your bonsai, so long as you're able to bend the branches. Typically, they're either copper or aluminum. Both of these will allow for the necessary force while being easy to apply. We'll talk more about choosing the right wire in Chapter Nine.

Bending Clamps

When you want more dramatic bends to your tree's aesthetic, you might use bending clamps. These allow for the branch to be repositioned gradually with a slight adjustment each day. Typically, they'll have two hooks that hold onto the tree and pull it and a foot that pushes where you want the bend. You then give the clamp one twist of the screw to increase pressure and shape the branches where you want them to be. They can come in many different sizes, so you'll be able to pick and choose the right size for your particular setting.

BONSAI

Chapter Summary

In this chapter, we went over some of the most important tools that you'll need in order to take care of your bonsai. These tools are some of the most common ones that you can expect to need.

- Never use your shears as wire cutters.

- Use the proper tool for the proper application so you can be sure you don't do unnecessary damage.

- Research is essential to know you've got a high-quality tool.

Next, we're going to address the different types of bonsai so you can start choosing the right kind.

CHAPTER FOUR

TYPES OF BONSAI

There is no one-size-fits-all approach to choosing the bonsai tree of your dreams. Just about any tree can be trained into the bonsai style if you're patient and diligent enough with your routine. The more that you work on pruning, confinement, and shaping, the easier it'll be to turn your plant into the look of your dreams.

While you can train just about anything, there are some species that are much more suited to training. As we go through this chapter, we're going to consider eight popular species, giving you all information you'll need to care for your trees. Some species may be more aesthetic than others, and some may be more resilient than others. Ultimately, to choose the right type of bonsai, you'll need to consider your own skill level and balance it out with the aesthetic that you're looking to get. The different looks will determine how you create the result.

BONSAI

Cedar

Cedar trees are quite dramatic thanks to their little needles and the ability to style them in several different ways. However, they're also somewhat challenging to grow on your own. These trees require experience to grow well, so if you're going into it as a beginner, be prepared for a lot of learning. You'll need to have the patience to work with your tree until it grows into what you want.

With the cragged-looking bark and short clusters of needles across the canopy, these looks are beautiful but so difficult to cultivate. They are tricky to grow, which makes them hard to find in shops. If you can find one and have the patience to prune and train it, you'll discover that it is actually quite satisfying.

Caring for Your Bonsai

Light Requirement: Minimal; your cedar bonsai needs about six hours of sunlight each day. They may be grown inside or outside, but when outdoors, make sure it isn't somewhere too sunny.

Temperature Tolerance: These plants do well with most outdoor weather, but when it starts dropping below around 40–45 degrees, you should probably bring it indoors.

Watering: Your bonsai will need watering regularly, but be careful to avoid overwatering it. When the foliage turns yellow, it's typically due to overwatering. Use soil that will allow for water to absorb but also be drained easily. Water when the soil is semi-dry.

Fertilizing: Your cedar tree news to be fertilized when you start seeing new springtime growths. Water immediately, and stop fertilizing when no new growth appears on the tree for the year.

Shaping: In order to shape your cedar bonsai, it's recommended that you pinch instead of prune. However, it grows so slowly that you usually don't have to do much with it. Use clean clippers when you do prune it. You can wire this tree easily at any stage in development, including into the desirable cascading style. Allow the wires to remain for at least two years, so the branches are trained properly. It's recommended that you choose copper wires.

Repotting: Your plant will need to be repotted sometimes; however, they really don't like the process. It's recommended to repot every five years or so, and do so in the springtime with acidic soil.

Pests and Concerns: Cedar bonsais often suffer from a few common diseases and pests that can be problematic. Keep an eye out for the following:

Mold and root rot: These primarily happen if you overwater your tree. The roots will drown and rot. Make sure you don't overwater and drain the soil if you have too much water.

Caterpillars: If your tree is outdoors, caterpillars will try to sneak onto it and eat it. Remove them whenever you see them.

Mites: Mites will also attempt to enjoy your cedar's foliage. They're hard to spot, but when you see one, there are probably many more.

BONSAI

Dwarf Jade

Jade trees, native to South Africa, have become incredibly popular in the bonsai world because they're so simple to keep alive. They're considered beautiful with their thick, brown stems and deep, thick oval-shaped leaves. These plants, which are technically succulents, are capable of creating beautiful, pink-tipped white star-shaped blossoms in the winter when they lack sunlight. However, keeping your plant indoors makes it difficult for

BONSAI

the plant to sense when it's time to flower. Get the blossoming effect by keeping this plant in full daylight outside starting in the fall.

Caring for Your Bonsai

Light Requirement: These plants are very versatile and can survive in anything from full sun to partial shade, so long as other conditions are met.

Temperature Tolerance: These plants tend to do well in temperatures between 70 and 75F during the daytime and 50–55° F at night.

Watering: As these plants are succulents, they don't need much water. They conserve water in their leaves and can tolerate not being watered daily. Typically, it's recommended that you water every 10–20 days, dropping down to just once a month waterings in the winter months.

Fertilizing

Shaping: When you shape your jade tree, you can use wires and prune to great success. The plants are perfectly happy being trained via wiring and will usually adapt to the new position within a month. Pruning should happen in the spring and summer so the plant can heal quicker. Cut right above the node where your plant is to get the best success.

Repotting: These plants grow slowly, and they'll typically dwarf when kept in a small pot. Repot when you want them in a larger container.

BONSAI

Pests and Concerns: These plants are typically susceptible to a few pests, including:

- **Mealybugs:** These bugs have a white, foamy appearance. They are easy to remove simply by treating the area with rubbing alcohol on cotton pads.

- **Aphids:** Aphids love jade plants and will pierce the leaves to suck out the sap. As they do so, they inject their own saliva inside the plant. They'll then leave behind a thick liquid called honeydew that coats the leaves and makes them appear sticky. This sticky liquid is dangerous and attracts ants and wasps to the area while leaving the plant susceptible to fungus.

Ficus

Ficus are incredibly popular bonsai trees thanks to their ornamental appearance. There are over 850 different

BONSAI

species available, and they typically all train well. These are common beginner options because of how well they respond to pruning and shaping. These plants grow naturally in hot, humid areas but are also adaptable enough that they can grow in shady areas as well.

These plants grow rapidly, spreading vertically and horizontally. They can branch out up to six feet per year in each direction, producing fruit as they do so. Thanks to how well they thrive, they're generally recognized as invasive. However, you should be able to grow them in a controlled manner if you're willing to keep them trimmed.

If you're a beginner, choose from many different species, but some of the most common are the weeping fig, the Morton Bay fig, and the Narrow Leaf fig. These plants should be grown indoors.

Caring for Your Bonsai

Light Requirement: These plants are meant to be indoor only to control their growth. Put them in a sunny place indoors where they will receive between six and eight hours of sunlight. If the leaves start yellowing, move it into a more indirect source.

Temperature Tolerance

Watering: These plants are tropical and love water. However, you need to be mindful not to overwater it. Make sure it can dry out between watering. Test this by pushing your finger through the soil. When it's dry all the way to the bottom, it's time to water it. Make sure that the water can drain out at the bottom, and don't let the soil remain dry for too long.

Ideally, you'll place your ficus's pot onto a tray filled with pebbles. As the water drains out of the pot and gets trapped by the tray, the water will evaporate and raise the humidity around the plant.

Fertilizing: This plant loves fertilizer when growing actively. Provide it with fertilizer every two weeks, switching between using a houseplant fertilizer and one that is high-nitrogen.

Shaping: You can shape your ficus relatively easily, but only when you do so early on. Wire your branches early on, when they are less than ½ inch thick, for the best results. Make it a point to remove wires when you're done with them and check on the wired branches regularly. Ficus can grow a great deal, so you need to avoid cuts or scars in the bark. Pruning the plant is easy, and you can do it at any time in the year. It will usually tolerate aggressive pruning.

Repotting: You need to repot healthy ficus bonsai plants every other year. You don't necessarily have to do so on a rigid schedule, but keep in mind that these plants are prone to having sudden growth spurts every now and then. If you notice that it's already gotten large, you can repot it early.

Pests and Concerns: These plants are quite hardy, and you're not likely to have too many problems with them.

BONSAI

Leaf drop: This happens when the plant starts shedding leaves. This happens commonly when the air is too cold. The plant could be in an area that is drafty or chilly. You may need to move it somewhere warmer, but the plant should be fine.

Root rot: Like so many other varieties of bonsai, ficus plants can be prone to root rot when you leave them immersed in too much water.

Japanese Maple

Seeing a Japanese maple growing in all its glory is a beautiful sight, with its red foliage ablaze and branches twisting in the air. These are one of the most popular trees and are the ones that most people picture when they imagine a bonsai tree. Thankfully, they're also quite easy to grow and are perfect beginner's trees. They don't require much on your end and can grow well indoors or outdoors, though they prefer outside in a sunny environment.

These trees are native to Japan, and as they mature, the leaves change colors dramatically. They begin growing in greenish and can turn to orange and red as they grow. The branches are quite suitable for training, and they respond well.

Caring for Your Bonsai

Light Requirement: They love light and do well with 8+ hours as long as they don't get too hot.

Temperature Tolerance: These plants are able to tolerate summer weather but don't do well when exposed to direct sunlight for long. The mature trees may be able to endure freezing conditions for a period but need to be protected from frost.

Watering: This tree should be kept evenly moist, and you should frequently water it from mid-spring to late summer. During the winter months, only water it when it's necessary to prevent it from becoming dry.

Fertilizing: Japanese maples do well with fertilizer every two weeks during the spring and summer. In the fall months, find a fertilizer that's nitrogen-free and don't feed them during the winter.

BONSAI

Shaping: These plants do well with shaping. You can reduce the size of the leaves by pruning them when they're in active growth. This will also boost the intensity of the coloration your leaves have in the fall. Pinch off new shoots to keep the plant in the style you've chosen. You can prune the main branches during the wintertime. They can be wired if necessary, and it should happen in the summertime. Don't leave the wiring on for more than six months, or you can cause problems with the bark.

Repotting: Your plant will need to be repotted once per year when they're young, and at ten years, they will need to be repotted every three years. Make sure you do this in the springtime before the leaf buds open up.

Pests and Concerns: These trees are quite hardy, but they have their fair share of weaknesses. In particular, they need to have plenty of ventilation, so they don't develop mildew.

BONSAI

Japanese Flowering Cherry

The Japanese cherry tree is gorgeous in the springtime as the blossoms sprout. These gorgeous ornamental trees are reminiscent of the beauty of spring, especially when the petals slowly drift to the ground. These trees, commonly called Japanese cherry blossom trees or sakura trees, are some of the most popular bonsai trees. With over 400 varieties to choose from, the most common is the Prunus serrulata.

In spring, they create beautiful pink and white blossoms. They've got dark horizontal lines along the

BONSAI

trunk as well. These plants aren't too difficult to grow, especially if you already know what you're doing.

Caring for Your Bonsai

Light Requirement: They need full sun, especially when growing. They need sunlight during spring and summer, so place them outdoor during these times to ensure they get the light they need.

Temperature Tolerance: They are quite tolerant to warmth but need to be dormant in the winter for three months. You can place them into a cold garage to trigger this.

Watering: Your plant will need regular watering so the soil never dries out entirely. When the soil starts looking dry, you should provide it with more water.

Fertilizing: Fertilize your plant once per month to nourish it using a balanced NPK fertilizer.

Shaping: These plants are typically quite resilient. However, you should only prune them after flowers have fallen, and, when possible, you should prune without removing new growth entirely. It is tolerant to wires and clamps, but remember to use aluminum wires because they are easier to manipulate and are softer.

Repotting: Your bonsai will need to be repotted sometimes, and the best time to do this is during the winter months. Use high-quality organic soil for this.

Pests and Concerns: Like most bonsai, your cherry blossom tree could be overwatered, causing root rot. Likewise, several pests will be happy to enjoy your plant's leaves as a quick snack, including spider mites, caterpillars, and other pests that find their way inside.

Juniper

Juniperus, commonly called the juniper, cover over 50 different evergreen coniferous shrubs and trees. They are

BONSAI

popular, as any variety of juniper is easy to train into a bonsai. They're naturally good picks for a few key reasons. Their foliage is naturally small, so they match up with the aesthetics of most miniature bonsais easily. They're also incredibly hardy and will do just fine under pruning, even if you get aggressive with it. However, these trees don't really do well indoor. Your juniper bonsai will do much better if you leave it outside and keep the soil dry. They come in several different color varieties, from yellow to dark green and just about anywhere in between.

These trees tend to have a rich, red hue that is commonly used in cabinetry. The berries produced by many junipers are used as a flavor for gin and get used regularly in Scandinavian dishes. They are among the easiest bonsai to grow, thanks to their durability.

Caring for Your Bonsai

Light Requirement: The bonsai tree does well with afternoon shade. It needs sunlight early on in the day but prefers not to be constantly left out in the sun. Aim for between four and eight hours of sunlight.

Temperature Tolerance:

Watering: This tree prefers to dry out between watering. Water should always be able to drain out the bottom of the pot to prevent the roots from rotting. Determine if they need water by taking a wooden chopstick or skewer and inserting it two inches into the soil. Wait ten minutes and check the surface of the wood.

BONSAI

If it's damp, don't bother with more water. If it's dry, it's time to add more water.

Humidity: Your plant will need humidity. Your pot should not be engulfed in water but should also be placed somewhere that it can get the right amount. Too much will rot your roots, and not enough will cause the roots to dry up and die. Place a humidity tray underneath the juniper bonsai without submerging the pot.

Fertilizing: Your juniper bonsai should be fertilized every three weeks, and in the spring, make sure that you choose one that is high in nitrogen. Summertime fertilizer should be more balanced. In the fall, use low-nitrogen fertilizer, and you can skip fertilization in the winter months. However, even though you don't fertilize in winter, you still need to water it.

Shaping: You can wire your juniper if you're careful. However, you need to take care of the tree and protect it from damage. Shape the juniper by heavily pruning and pinching off new shoots at one inch long at the start of spring.

Repotting: Your plant needs to be repotted every two years. Older trees can go a bit longer without repotting. When you do repot, avoid aggressive pruning of the roots. The containers will help to stunt the growth of the tree. Remember that you must prune the roots when you repot.

Pests and Concerns: These plants tend to be somewhat resistant to pests, though there are a few to be concerned about. The most common pests for concern in this species are:

- **Abiotic Maladies:** Abiotic means not alive. These trees are resilient, but when in the wrong environment for too long, they can suffer from abiotic maladies. Such instances include extreme weather, poor cultivation, and external damage.

- **Pests:** Junipers are typically resistant to pests, but if the foliage pads are too thick, you may find that the pests move in. Spider mites, juniper scale, juniper aphids, juniper webworms, and the like can cause an infestation that will eventually damage the tree.

Pine

Pines are incredibly common in the bonsai world. As evergreens, they've got their foliage year-round, and they bear cones and needles that can be a wonder to behold in all their glory. These plants can grow in several different

BONSAI

shapes. They can also be shaped into just about any style that is known to bonsai. They are the classic choice, commonly maintained for generations in families, passed down from person to person. With over 120 species to choose from, there are plenty of options that may work for you. The most common is the Japanese black pine, known for its black trunk.

Caring for Your Bonsai

Light Requirement: These plants require plenty of sunlight during spring, summer, and fall. Without enough light, the tree can be forced to elongate its needles while experiencing dieback of the branches that couldn't reach any sunlight.

Temperature Tolerance: These plants do well in most environments, but they can suffer when subjected to freezing winds. These plants typically like the outdoor weather, with some pines doing well even when the weather is freezing. Place it in the sunniest place you can in your yard during the summer months. In the winter, keep in mind that your plant's roots aren't as insulated as they'd be in the ground. The roots will likely freeze, and you'll want to shield them from wind during this time.

Watering: It can be somewhat tricky to water these trees. You need to give them plenty of water when they're close to drying out, but too much water is likely to cause them to develop root rot. They dislike both wet and dry roots, so you have to find a balance somewhere in the middle. Skipping watering can cause a lot of problems.

Make sure you check the soil's dryness a few times per day to keep it well-watered.

Fertilizing: These trees don't need too much in the way of fertilizer. Because these trees have their needles long-term, you don't usually have to worry about providing the energy they'll need to grow more. And, by limiting how much food you offer them, you'll also make it grow smaller needles. Feed it in early spring with 0-10-10 fertilizer, and again at the end of spring, then feed it a small amount of 12-10-10 fertilizer every two weeks until fall begins. Then, allow it to rest over the winter.

Shaping: Shaping your pine tree takes a lot of time and effort. They're known for the difficulty in pruning because, while the pruning itself is easy, the plant itself can be somewhat temperamental. They don't like change, and you have to acclimate them to it very slowly. Remove branches in the fall when it's beginning to enter dormancy, and you must leave these cuts covered up after you've made them. They will bleed sap upon cutting. However, by covering it with petroleum jelly, you can help keep the plant healthy. You then have to leave the stump alone to dry out for a year before total removal.

You also can't remove more than half of its growth in a year, or it may struggle. They often struggle if you dramatically change their environment more than once per year as well. So, for example, if you repot your plant one year, it probably won't tolerate heavy pruning as well.

BONSAI

Pests and Concerns: These plants are finicky, and if you mess with them too much, they're probably not going to be very happy. Keep this in mind when you grow them. Generally, pine bonsai trees are not recommended for beginners because of the work that goes into keeping them alive. However, they are some of the most popular.

BONSAI

Pomegranate

BONSAI

Fruiting trees can be trained into bonsai trees with plenty of success, and the pomegranate is a popular example of this. This deciduous tree drops most leaves over the winter without ever creating the vivid colors of fall leaves that we usually think of with deciduous species. Its flowers are capable of bearing fruit, and its trunk is usually thick, twisting naturally to get the ancient appearance that people usually attempt to foster with their bonsai trees. These plants are native to the Mediterranean and, thus, are more successful in similar climates. They prefer to be kept warm and comfortable.

Caring for Your Bonsai

Light Requirement: These plants love sunny, warm weather with plenty of light and shade in the winter.

Temperature Tolerance: Bonsai readily tolerate regions similar in temperature and climate to the Mediterranean. Otherwise, they are best grown indoors.

Watering: These trees need to be watered regularly in order to keep the soil moist but not wet. Make sure you don't water so much in the winter. They tend to appreciate being misted in the winter months.

Fertilizing: You will need to fertilize your tree every other week, especially in spring. Make a point of using liquid fertilizer and adding organic fertilizer. Remember not to fertilize for the first three months after repotting.

Shaping: You will need to work to keep your tree shaped well. This can be done with regular pinching of the first or third leaf so you can encourage young shoots to mature rather than growing more. You should avoid wiring these plants; instead, prioritize shaping and using clips. New growth thickens quickly, so it's important to prevent scarring by not wiring it too much.

Repotting: If you're looking for blooms, they do the best when the plants are restricted by the pot. You should only repot every three or four years to allow for emphasis on bloom growth. When the time to repot comes, make sure you only do so late in winter and provide your plant soil that is high in sand and lime.

Pests and Concerns: Either indoors or outdoors, these plants are vulnerable to pests. In particular, look out for the following:

- **Whiteflies:** If you're indoors, you may find that you foster these pests. Provide plenty of ventilation while also spritzing the bottom of your leaves with water.

- **Aphids:** Aphids love to drink the juice of these leaves. You can rinse them off with water, or you can provide natural predators, such as ladybugs, to take care of them.

- **Mold:** Mold can be a huge problem for these trees if not treated well. Make sure that you prevent this by not overwatering your plants while still providing plenty of ventilation.

BONSAI

Other Favorite Bonsai Species

While the previously listed trees are some of the most popular choices for bonsai trees, there really is no shortage of a variety out there for you. You can choose from all sorts of different trees, and chances are, you would probably be able to turn it into a bonsai at some point. However, it may require plenty of care to do so. Let's go over a few honorable mentions.

Apple trees

Just about any apple tree can be turned into a bonsai. With the right care, they can develop their beautiful flowers and then produce mini fruits, the size of coins, if you've provided them with what they need.

Azalea trees

If you're looking for fragrant, floral trees, this is a wonderful choice. With their bright pink blossoms and small leaves, azalea trees are easily trained. They can look like either trees or shrubs, and they are absolutely breathtaking when in bloom. Even when not in bloom, the small eaves lend themselves perfectly to the aesthetic of bonsai trees.

Bamboo

While bamboo may not be particularly conventional, some types of bamboo are well-suited to bonsai. In particular, heavenly bamboo can be shaped into the look of a beautiful tree.

Money tree

While you may not have thought of those little money tree plants that you can buy at most plant shops as a bonsai, they are one. These trees can be trained to grow indoors in beautiful patterns, and it is also believed that money trees bring good luck.

Honeysuckle

The honeysuckle tree can produce vibrant blossoms with deep, verdant green leaves that can be a true spectacle to behold. They love to grow out and require care to keep under control. However, they are well worth the effort, and if you provide enough sunlight, they are likely to be beautiful.

BONSAI

Chapter Summary

In this chapter, we've discussed the different types of bonsai trees. Specifically, we've covered the following topics:

- The most popular bonsai types;
- The characteristics and care needs of the most popular bonsai types;
- Other types of bonsai trees.

In the next chapter, you will learn about the styles of bonsai and what makes them so distinctive.

BONSAI

CHAPTER FIVE

BONSAI STYLES

Bonsai Chokkan style *Bonsai Bujingi style* *Bonsai Shakan style* *Bonsai Fukinagashi style*

Bonsai Soju style *Bonsai Sokan style* *Bonsai Sabamiki style* *Bonsai Moyogi style* *Bonsai Nejikan style*

Bonsai Neagari style *Bonsai Ishitzuki style* *Bonsai Sekijoju style* *Bonsai Han-Kengai style* *Bonsai Kengai style*

Bonsai trees are typically classified by style. Before you begin doing anything to a tree, you must first identify

BONSAI

the style that you want to follow and then shape it accordingly. There are many different configurations, but most tend to fall into one of several categories. Below, you'll be introduced to them in both English and Japanese names. Choose the right one for you from the different varieties. We'll be going over seven of the most common styles.

Classifications are made by analyzing the general shape of the tree and the way that the trunk slants with an invisible vertical axis. Of course, the starting point is how the tree will stand in the container of your choice. Before you start shaping, you must first imagine how your tree will look in the container itself. If your tree is going to slant, you need to plan accordingly to make sure that your pot doesn't appear unbalanced. An upright tree should look stable, and slanted or cascaded styles should have root surfaces visible. No matter how you choose to plant, it's important to imagine your bonsai's final form before you begin anything. Have a plan before you get started, and you'll save yourself a lot of heartbreak from making a mistake along the way.

Formal Upright (Chokkan)

The formal upright bonsai is a classic bonsai and is the most basic form a bonsai can take. This means that it's also one of the most beginner-friendly because it's relatively simple to maintain. You don't have to experiment to get branches going where you want them, and you won't really need to worry so much about selective pruning. You'll also have the added benefit of acknowledging that you should be able to display your bonsai almost immediately.

This style is usually either conical or rounded, with the leader and horizontal branches erect. One of the branches is typically slightly lower than the other and will extend further from the trunk than other branches will. The two lowest branches must be trained to point toward the front. The third branch then extends back, somewhere between the first two branches' heights, to create depth.

If you choose to select a nursery plant in this style, you want to look to the trunk first. The trunk should be straight and without forks. They should have a balanced distribution of all branches, with the first of them already at the right position around a third of the way up the trunk.

Typically, it's best to avoid fruiting or trees that are naturally more varied in their symmetry. Conifers are among the easiest to maintain. Remember that you don't need perfect symmetry, just balance.

Recommended Species

Spruces, pines, junipers, larches, maples (with extra training).

Recommended Containers

Oval or rectangular containers. Plant it about a third from the end of the container to prevent too much symmetry.

BONSAI

Informal Upright (Moyogi)

The informal upright bonsai tree is similar to the first but is a bit more relaxed. The tree's trunk is allowed to bend slightly in the front to create a slight slant of the tree. The trunk should still appear to be a line, with a slight bend to it. The line should be from tip to roots, with the in-between being allowed some flexibility, so long as the slant is toward the front.

Branching with this type of plant should start roughly a third of the way up the trunk with few empty spaces left behind. Check if a nursery tree is a good pick for an informal upright tree by looking at it from above. If it doesn't look appealing, you'll need to move the rootball so you can slant the tree differently.

Recommended Species

Most trees are acceptable choices here. Most common include the Japanese maple, trident maple, conifers, crab apple, pomegranate, cotoneaster, and beech trees.

Recommended Containers

This tree looks best by using similar planting techniques to the formal upright. Choose something that is oval or rectangular and plant the tree slightly to the side.

Slanting (Shakan)

Slanting trees are trees that have been caused to grow somewhat slanted by nature. Usually, wind or gravity takes its hold and forces the tree in a sideways growth instead of straight and upright. Non-vertical growth causes the branches to reach out horizontally. These can be impressive to behold, appearing to be older and stronger. Typically, there is a sharp bend somewhere in the tree, with the slant moving toward the front. The lowest branch should always point in the direction that is opposite the bend. Lower branches should be in threes at a third of the way up the trunk mark.

This tree is basically a compromise between the cascade and the upright trees, with the balance being found between the trunk's movement and branches to create a sense that the tree is not lopsided.

Recommended Species

Most species. Conifers are among the best. Other common choices include the Japanese maple, trident maple, crabapple, pomegranate, cotoneaster, and beech trees.

Recommended Containers

Typically, these trees look the best when they're put in round or square containers, right in the center.

Cascade (Kengai)

The cascade bonsai appears like a tree that has grown downward on an embankment. Typically, the trunk begins upward, growing out of the soil, but then reaches downward suddenly, with the bottom positioned beneath the end of the container. The container is often placed on a stand or table, so the tree's foliage is free to grow downward.

Typically, most foliage in this tree appears underneath the soil's surface on a vertical plane. It is a difficult tree to train and can take much longer than creating a slanting style. Typically, it's recommended that you choose a tree that grows low naturally rather than attempting to force an upright tree to bend unnaturally. One of the back branches should be vertical, and the side branches should flow naturally.

Recommended Species

Be careful here, as some trees that go upright might resist styling. Conifers tend to yield good luck, along with ficus trees.

Recommended Containers

Typically, these trees are placed in either round or hexagonal containers that have more height than width.

Semi-Cascade (Han-Kengai)

The semi-cascade bonsai tree shows an upright trunk that grows straight, then cascades at a gentler slope than the cascade style. Typically, the trunk curves and doesn't quite reach the bottom of the container like the cascade tree does. These branches are typically in the front of the tree. Branches and foliage should be underneath the soil line but not underneath the bottom of the container.

Recommended Species

These plants require pots that are either round, hexagonal, or square. The pots should be a bit deeper than they are wide.

Recommended Containers

Any plants that are commonly used for cascade trees should work well. You may also want to try prostrate junipers or flowering plants for good results.

Windswept (Fukinagashi)

The windswept look is supposed to be off-balance. It is meant to look like the branches have been exposed to strong winds that have forced the branches to be swept to one side. These trees are usually designed to look like coastal or mountain trees that have spent a lifetime being sculpted by nature. They are quite striking to behold but also can be difficult to achieve. Typically, these trees are the most reminiscent of the original penzai trees that had been spotted in China. They are typically seen as a bit cruder but are also among the more difficult ones to create, as you cannot display scars from removing branches on the side of the bonsai. You have to be able to train it to not only bend like it is being bent by the wind, but you have to also make sure that the foliage appears to be windswept as well.

Recommended Species

Chinese elm is the most traditional of the windswept trees, but most trees should train just fine in this style.

Recommended Containers

These are usually planted in square planters, with the trunk being on one point while the bend goes opposite it.

Literati (Bunjin)

Literati bonsai trees are unlike most other trees that you're likely to see. They are commonly spoken of as "refined elegance" in an attempt to describe them. They are different from anything found in nature, and yet, they take on an air of elegance in their own right. They commonly have trunks that have been trained to twist and turn in several curves, with trunks that remain narrow and no lower branches. They are somewhat like the informal upright trees, but not quite.

Literati bonsai trees lack patterns but have their own set form. They look as if they are struggling and deformed, and yet, the trees should be healthy. They are rare due to their unconventional shape and size, and yet they are worthy of respect.

Recommended Species

Typically, conifers do the best with this intense, rigorous training. Deciduous trees struggle but are possible.

Recommended Containers

Because of all of the movement in the trunk, these plants usually need a shallow round or oval container or a tray with stone. This design is meant to be simple, so you ought to choose planters that are simple as well.

BONSAI

Chapter Summary

In this chapter, we've discussed the various bonsai styles. Specifically, we've covered the following topics:

- The major group styles;
- The purposes of the style categorization system;
- The styles within each major group style;
- Miscellaneous other styles.

In the next chapter, you will learn about the various types of bonsai trees.

CHAPTER SIX

CHOOSING YOUR BONSAI TREE

Before you choose your bonsai tree, consider several important issues. After all, if it were as simple as picking

BONSAI

out a tree with an aesthetic you enjoy and then letting it grow and trimming every one and then, you probably wouldn't need a book to guide you! When you're deciding upon the perfect tree to use for your own bonsai, several different factors will help you to figure out what it is that you really want out of your tree. From deciding that you need something that's easy or needs to be left outdoors or choosing something with flowers, you need to think about what your current requirements and restrictions are and then work to find a tree that fits your needs.

As you consider these, you're bound to start figuring out what it is that you need in a tree, and that will help you to recognize your limits. From there, we'll go over some of the most important steps to finding the best tree when it's time to buy one. While each tree will look a little different, and there will be differences here and there, there are still important ways that you can ensure that a tree you're choosing is healthy enough to transform into a bonsai. These trees take a long time to train and cultivate, so it's important to choose a healthy base.

Where Will Your Tree Grow?

One question to ask yourself before anything else is where your tree will grow. Do you want an indoor or outdoor tree? Do you want something that you can display indoors, all year? Or would you prefer to have something that grows outdoors only? This determines the options you've got, especially when you start considering what your environment looks like.

If you want to have an outdoor tree, you need to consider what your weather and climate is like. If you want to grow a tree that requires heavy overwintering in an area where temperatures rarely drop below 60 °F, there's a chance you're going to run into problems. Likewise, if you choose something that needs tropical weather to grow and you live in an area that gets all four seasons, including a snowy winter, your tree won't be happy.

Bonsais are smaller than full-grown trees, and, because of their size and because they grow above ground, they tend to be more sensitive to temperatures. This means that you need to take care of them carefully. Indoor-only trees will usually do fine as long as you can keep an appropriate environment. Some trees may prefer to be outdoors, and if your climate doesn't match what they require, you should probably skip the variety. Get to know the particular species that you want to grow, and compare its requirements to what you can provide before deciding what to grow.

Size of Your Desired Tree

You should also consider what size you want your tree to be. It's possible to have large bonsai trees, with the imperial size being up to 80 inches tall, so consider what the size of your tree will be. Indoor trees are best kept to smaller proportions, while outdoor trees can grow larger. When you want to include a large tree, you'll also need a species that naturally grows larger as well.

Style Chosen for Your Bonsai

You should also figure out what kind of bonsai tree you want to grow. Is there a specific pattern and style you'd like to train your tree into? Most deciduous trees, for example, don't tend to work well with cascading styles. If you have a specific style in mind before you begin choosing a tree, you can use that to guide your decision.

Your Skill Level

Consider your skill level before you pick out a tree. Your skill level will determine the kind of tree you select. While some trees may be stunning, they may not be very beginner-friendly. The truth is, when you're a beginner, you'll make mistakes—there's no way around it. When you're learning a craft, you'll have to practice it before you have the skills solidified. You're going to need to practice well before you take on something like pine.

Some trees are naturally more resistant to mistakes. If you mess up, they won't necessarily die. Others may struggle to recover from a mistake. A lot of time and effort goes into raising a bonsai, so you don't want to choose a tree that is going to die the first time you do something wrong, especially if you've never raised one before. This is where choosing something within your experience level is important.

How to Choose the Right Tree

When it's time to start choosing your own tree, start by narrowing down the right choice with several important steps. A bonsai tree is a reflection of you, so choose a tree

BONSAI

that resonates with you. You need something that, when you look at it, reminds you of why you want to make a bonsai tree in the first place. When you've narrowed down the species, it's time to start selecting the exact tree that you'll cultivate into your own personal masterpiece.

Starter Trees, Cuttings, and Seeds

You've got three primary options when you're going to start your own bonsai tree. You can choose a tree that has already been trained so you can perfect it into your exact vision. You can choose to create something that has grown from a cutting and has been able to grow roots. Alternatively, you can also grow a tree from a seed, being able to change it from the very beginning.

Growing from seed will take a long while. It takes at least three years before your seedling is large enough to start shaping at all, and it will be around 15 years before it's considered fully grown. However, growing from seed allows you to maintain complete control over the plant and its growth.

Choosing from cuttings is a good way to find a middle ground, but it still takes time for your plant to really start branching out enough to grow and shape.

Typically, beginners are encouraged to start with a starter tree that has already gone through those first few stages. That way, you're able to start determining the shape and the way that you choose to train it. And, because there is probably already some degree of training done, you should find it easier to manage.

Checking the Health

When you're looking for a tree to grow and foster, the best starting point is a local nursery. This will let you see the trees face to face. You also get the added benefit of knowing that if it's growing in a local nursery, it should probably grow well in your environment as well.

When looking at potential trees, pay attention to the general health of the tree. Are there pests or diseases? Do you see signs of yellowing or a general lack of health? How are the branches? The trunk should be thicker than the branches, and the branches themselves should be strongly positioned and more or less where you'd want them on your tree. They should already be naturally symmetrical and balanced to have a good chance at becoming a healthy bonsai.

Finally, consider plants that are healthy-looking off the bat. They should look like their foliage is coming in completely and healthily. Signs of yellowing are generally a sign that the tree is unhealthy.

BONSAI

Chapter Summary

In this chapter, we've discussed what to consider when choosing the bonsai tree that is right for you and the pot to grow it in. Specifically, we've covered the following topics:

- Where you will grow the tree;
- The size of your tree;
- The health of your tree;
- The style that you will apply;
- Your expertise and knowledge;
- How to pick out the right tree.

In the next chapter, you will learn about the tools you need to cultivate bonsai.

CHAPTER SEVEN

CULTIVATING YOUR BONSAI

When you're ready to start cultivating your bonsai tree, you need to know how to take care of it. To cultivate your tree is to care for it; it is to be able to provide what is necessary to change the shape of the tree into what you desire for it to become. Cultivation is usually used to describe the practice of producing food through preparing the land to grow crops, but in this case, we talk about bonsai as that which is being cultivated.

Cultivate your bonsai by meeting several key criteria. You will need to provide the right soil for the particular tree you've chosen. You'll need to choose the right container to allow it to grow while also paying attention to the shape of the container in regards to the plant's needs and the aesthetic you're going for. You'll also need to understand how to fertilize, water, and care for your plant by providing it with the right care.

We'll also consider the propagation of your bonsai tree. Maybe you want to grow another one from your tree for someone else. Or maybe you just want to know how you can grow your own bonsai from a seed or cutting. Either way, being able to encourage propagation is an important skill to learn. This chapter is here to provide you with the necessary skills to provide expert care for your tree so you can rest assured knowing that it will be healthy. Upon establishing the essentials to keeping your plants alive, we'll then start delving into how to shape your tree in future chapters.

Soil

Your first inclination upon getting a bonsai might be to put it in a pot with potting soil. After all, it's a plant in a pot, right? Shouldn't that naturally be what you do to keep it growing properly? The problem is, this isn't accurate at

BONSAI

all. Soil for bonsais is actually a bit different because you're not just allowing for the growth of a plant; you're growing a *tree*.

Soil may not be particularly interesting, but it is crucial to ensure that you have the right kind of soil if you want to grow healthy bonsais. We tend to plant bonsais in containers with less space than most plants normally get, so the soil quality is even more essential. If something is off balance, there's a much larger chance that your plant is going to suffer for it.

Your tree uses soil to accomplish a few different jobs. It helps the plant to build a steady support system that it can use to keep balance. In the ground, trees dig their root systems down to cement themselves deeply enough to keep upright. They do the same thing in their containers, so you need to provide them with enough soil to support them.

Soil Requirements

The soil must meet three key criteria if it is to be good enough for your bonsai: sufficient water retention, aeration, and drainage. Your tree's roots need to be able to absorb water to pull in the hydration and minerals it needs. Most bonsai don't take too kindly to being fully submerged in water or being dried out. So, prevent these problems by using soil that will hold enough water within it to keep the roots satisfied while still providing enough space for air pockets. The aeration allows for the roots to get enough air that will help them to avoid drowning. Yes, your tree's

BONSAI

roots need oxygen! Make sure that the soil allows for sufficient drainage, so you know that the water isn't going to get stuck around the roots. As a result, you'll find the roots are kept healthier. In those air holes, you'll also see the development of micro-bacteria that are important for your plants to thrive as well.

What Is Soil Made From?

There are many different types of soil. It can be clay, mulchy, sandy, or silty. The various kinds of soil are important and different plants require different needs. When it comes to bonsai trees, typically, they need to meet certain criteria. Bonsai soil should be pH-neutral most of the time, which means that it is neither basic nor acidic. Some plants do well with acidities, such as many that produce fruits and vegetables. However, bonsai want to be kept at a neutral 6.5 to 7.5 pH to grow healthily.

The soils advertised for bonsais are typically made of:

- **Akadama:** This is a type of hard-baked Japanese clay you can buy online if you can't find it locally. It's used to create extra aeration. However, after a few years, it starts losing its structure, which can lead to problems with aeration being lost. You can either use akadama with several other well-draining options or replace the soil and repot every couple of years.

- **Pumice:** This is a soft product that is meant to absorb water and nutrients, so they're available for your tree when needed. It helps to boost water retention without being soggy.

- **Organic potting compost:** This compost could be all sorts of different things. It's commonly made of perlite, peat moss, and sand. It's not supposed to aerate or drain well because it's used in tandem with other components that will aerate. It is meant to absorb the water. Commonly, people enjoy using pine bark, which will break down slowly.

- **Fine gravel:** Often, people like to put a layer of gravel or sand across the bottom of the container because this will allow for further drainage. This is becoming more and more uncommon but is a good idea to consider, especially if you want to mix in lava rock with a mixture of akadama, soil, and pumice.

Making Your Own Bonsai Soil

If you want to make your own bonsai soil, there are a few guidelines that you can use based on the types of trees you're using. However, these are general and meant to cover a wide range of trees. If you know that your tree likes different soil, you should use that instead. However, in a pinch when you're not sure what to do, you can use these soil guidelines:

For deciduous trees: ½ akadama, ¼ pumice, ¼ lava rock

For conifer trees: ⅓ akadama, ⅓ pumice, ⅓ lava rock

You may also need to make some considerations based on your area. For example, if you want to have wetter soil, you could add in more akadama and potting compost to boost water retention. Living somewhere wetter would probably require you to make some changes to allow for better drainage of the soil.

When you're mixing your soil, make sure you first allow the dust from the akadama to be sifted. Then, mix in the pumice, and finally, add in the lava rock. If you need more water absorption, toss in organic soil. If a soil mix doesn't seem quite right, don't feel discouraged! You can continue to tweak it until you find the right mix for you. It's normal for there to be some trial and error to perfect it.

Choosing the Deep Enough Container

In bonsai, the container is as important as the tree itself. They work in harmony with each other, and you'll need to choose the right pot to convey the message you'd like to show. Many important factors come into consideration when choosing a container, but we will get into this later. For now, the only factor that matters is the pot's depth. We will delve into choosing the right sizes, colors, textures, and more while discussing how to show off your tree later.

The dimension you choose for your container is entirely dependent upon the tree you've chosen and how

BONSAI

big it has gotten. While choosing a container that's too big is technically not a problem for the health of your plants, it does make a difference in the aesthetic.

One of the most important parts of choosing the right size container is ensuring that it's deep enough. Calculate the depth by looking at the diameter of the tree just above the soil. However, several plants might require something that is deeper. Always be well-informed of the particular species you've chosen.

Fertilizing

Your plant has to be fed. While plants do use photosynthesis to create their own energy source, they still need vitamins and minerals so they can grow properly. Your body needs vitamins and minerals to grow faster, and your tree needs these as well. Primarily, it gets its needs from the soil, but when you have your plant growing in such a confined space, that plant can't dig deeper with its roots to find new sources. In this case, the next best thing is to provide fertilization to your plant in other ways. In this section, it's important to look at what your plants need as well as when and how to fertilize them.

The Purpose of Fertilization

Fertilization of your soil is essential to provide your plants with the nutrients they need to grow. As already mentioned, normal, full-sized trees compensate for their nutritional needs by digging deeper and further into the soil. This isn't an option for plants that live in containers.

This is where fertilizer comes into play. Fertilizers will provide all essential vitamins and minerals used to turn carbon dioxide and water into the sugars used for energy. Just about any fertilizer that you purchase is going to provide all the important elements your plants will need. In particular, you'll see nitrogen, phosphorus, and potassium emphasized as macronutrients; they are essential for full, healthy growth.

Fertilizers will come in powdered or liquid form. Because your soil doesn't have access to the natural organic manner that would normally fertilize it, and because your tree can't dig more, you'll have to add these nutrients in other ways.

NPK Numbers

While there are several important vitamins and minerals, the three most important are nitrogen, phosphorus, and potassium. Each of these three elements is critical for your bonsai to grow. Most growth problems come from missing one of these three things. When you get a fertilizer, you'll see three numbers on it, such as 10-9-8. What this tells you is that the fertilizer is 10% nitrogen, 9% phosphorus, and 8% potassium. You can get these in different ratios, and depending upon the plant, how it's growing, or what it's designed to do, you'll need to provide different levels of nutritional value. For example, flowering and fruiting plants are going to require higher levels of nutrients to grow.

Nitrogen

Nitrogen is essential to plant growth. It is necessary for the growth and development of the leaves.

Phosphorus

Phosphorus is necessary for the development of roots, flowers, and fruit development.

Potassium

Potassium is essential for the general functionality of the plant.

When to Fertilize

Fertilizing your trees should happen at different points in time. Certain plants require regular feeding, while others may want to be left unfed over time. Because of the many different types of bonsais, you'll need to ensure yours is just right for whatever type of tree you've chosen.

As a general guideline, you can more or less generalize how often you'll need to fertilize your plant based on the type of tree it is.

Deciduous Trees

Deciduous trees require regular fertilization to allow for their leaves to develop and grow. However, as soon as they're no longer filled with leaves, the feeding should slow down. Focus on feeding the deciduous trees weekly during the spring and summer months. Then, as the trees lose their leaves, you can provide a 0-10-0 fertilizer until all leaves have fallen off, at which point you can wait until spring.

Conifer Bonsai Trees

Conifer trees maintain their foliage long-term. Fertilize these trees weekly during the growth period, and you'll need to provide their nutrients in the winter as well. Provide them with nutrients at least once per month throughout the winter.

Tropical or Subtropical Trees

Tropical and subtropical trees require lots of nourishment during the growing season. Feed them monthly from fall to spring and weekly the rest of the year.

Liquid vs. Slow-Release Fertilizers

You've got so many different options that you can use to fertilize. You could, for example, choose a liquid fertilizer that you can use to water your plants. Alternatively, with bonsai trees, you can also create the right environment through the use of slow-release pellets that slowly release their nutrients into the soil for your tree to absorb. As the trees absorb the nutrients, you'll need to add them back in again. Make sure that you remember to continue adding them. Starving your trees of fertilizers is not going to help them to grow. The only real difference between the two types of fertilizers is how you apply them and how long they last. It's up to personal preference if you'd prefer to have it in liquid or pellet form.

How to Fertilize Your Tree

Fertilizing your tree is simple once you know what you're doing and have chosen the right one. Liquid fertilizers tend to be fast-acting but also need to be reapplied more often. Granular or pellet fertilizers are typically going to last longer in the soil before you need to replace them.

It's strongly recommended that you look at the fertilizer you've chosen and go over the instructions provided. You'll be able to fertilize, either by pushing the granulated fertilizer into the soil or mixing and pouring the fertilizer in the water.

Keep in mind that you should always follow the instructions on the fertilizer. You can absolutely over-fertilize, and if you do so, your plants are not going to live well. Too many nutrients can actually burn the plant and kill it quickly, as plants typically can't stop absorption from happening. If it's dissolved into the liquid, the roots are going to absorb them, even if it's too much.

What Makes a Good Fertilizer?

If you're wondering what makes a good fertilizer, you're in the right spot. The first time you buy a fertilizer can be incredibly intimidating, but once you find a good one, there's no reason to keep switching it up. The best fertilizers are made from high-quality ingredients. Ideally, they would be organic as opposed to chemical-based. Natural fertilizers are absorbed better.

BONSAI

Watering

Water is essential if you want your plant to grow. You may have a set way that you water your houseplants, but you'll need to water your bonsai differently. This is because your bonsai tree will have a smaller, compact, and confined root system that needs to be watered more often but in smaller quantities. You don't want to over-water the soil and let water get stuck, but you don't want to under-water the plants, either.

Different trees will obviously have different preferences, and you'll need to be able to water to their requirements. You'll need to be able to know how much water your plants will need and how you can provide that.

How Often You Should Water Your Bonsai

There is no one-size-fits-all watering schedule you can follow. However, you should make it a point to check your soil regularly to ensure that it has enough. By learning the signs and doing a bit of research about that particular plant that you're raising, you should be able to figure out how much water they need.

Push your finger into the soil to work out if your plant needs water. If you can't feel much water in the top part of the soil, then it's probably a good idea to add more water to the bonsai. However, some plants may not share the same sentiment. Jade plants, for example, love to be allowed to dry out a bit between watering, but pines won't tolerate the dryness.

BONSAI

Eventually, you'll be able to tell more about your unique plant. You'll be able to tell at a glance whether it needs to be watered by how the foliage looks or how light the pot feels. As you get better, you can start predicting when you need to water it.

How to Water Your Bonsai

When you need to water your plant, you've got two options. You can either use an overhead watering method or an immersion method. Each of these has its own benefits, and you'll have to pick and choose what to use and when.

The overhead watering method uses a hose, can, or something else to deliver the water from above. Pour the water into the soil, just as you would for other plants. However, you must make sure that you deliver the water gently. Otherwise, you could unintentionally dislodge or disturb the soil. Pour the water gently, and stop if it starts puddling up on the top until it has a chance to soak into the soil. Continue this until you see that the water is dripping out of the container and into the humidity tray.

The immersion method is slightly different but only really works for smaller trees that you can physically move. Take a bucket and fill it with water. The water needs to be deep enough so that when you insert the tree's pot into the water, you'll notice it bubbling. If it bubbles quickly, you haven't been watering enough. Immerse it until it no longer bubbles. Remove the tree and let it drain.

BONSAI

Should You Water All of Your Bonsai at the Same Time?

You might be tempted to use one bonsai as a determining factor for whether you should water all of them. However, this isn't a good idea. All plants have different containers, soil, and absorption speeds. It's better to check each tree individually before deciding to water them. This is especially the case in summer.

When Should You Water?

If you're wondering what time of the day is best for watering, you're asking a great question. Generally speaking, the only real rule is to avoid watering at the hottest point in the day when exposed to full sun. Late afternoon or early morning is usually a good time. Keep in mind that if your tree is in full light, you may need to water it multiple times daily during the heat of summer. However, make sure you don't get water on the leaves; this can cause the sunlight to burn the leaves.

What Kind of Water?

Use tap water if you want to. If your water is safe enough for you to drink, you should be able to use it for your trees as well. However, if you have hard water, you might notice white salt deposits. You can get rid of this by using collected rainwater, but it's not normally a big deal. If your water is chlorinated, you might want to let it sit out overnight to allow the chlorine to evaporate before you use it.

BONSAI

Misting Your Plant

Sometimes, your plant will appreciate a bit of a spritz every now and then. This will help to refresh foliage when it's starting to dry out a bit, but it isn't the same as watering. Bonsais require humidity to some degree, so you need to make sure that you spritz them if the indoor environment is getting too dry. In particular, think about the dryness in the room that's created in the winter by running your heater. This dryness can be brutal to your plants. Mist your plants by giving a gentle spritz over the leaves and boost humidity.

If you live in a particularly dry environment, there's an easy solution to this problem: making an evaporation tray. Do this by taking a flat tray that you've filled up with some rocks and water and place your pot on top of it. The water should not go all the way to the bottom of the tray, as you want to make sure that the soil can drain into the tray. As the water evaporates, you'll start to get the added benefit of humidity being created around your plants.

What About Vacations?

If you plan on traveling for several days or weeks, your trees won't do well without water. You'll need to provide it to them somehow, whether you get a friend to come over or leave your tree with a friend, so you know it gets watered.

You could also get a vacation drip, which is a watering tool that can allow a slow trickle of water to enter the soil.

However, if you're going to be gone for more than a few days, this isn't a recommended option. If your tree dries out, you can't just give it a few splashes of water and expect it to be fine, so you'll want to make sure it's cared for.

You could also wrap the bonsai's pot and soil into a plastic bag sealed tightly right after watering it well. Then, leave your bonsai somewhere cool and brightly lit while you're gone. Depending on how quickly your plant absorbs water, you may be able to leave it for several days.

Lighting

While you can grow a bonsai indoors, they definitely prefer to be outside in the natural sunlight. We can mimic natural sunlight relatively closely with grow lights but can't get it quite right. Nevertheless, using a grow light is a valid option indoors, depending upon the tree you choose.

Because bonsais require photosynthesis, they need a significant amount of sunlight to ensure they make enough energy for themselves. Choosing the right grow lights is the perfect way to ensure they're happy and healthy. You've got several different options, but the main three are fluorescent, HID, or LED lights.

Fluorescent Lights

Fluorescent lights are somewhat old-school, but they do get the job done. They come in a wide range of strengths and colors, and depending on the stage of your plant, you'll need different kinds of lights. For example, if you want healthy foliage, you need 6000K lights. For plants getting ready to bud and flower, you'll want to use 2700K bulbs. These lights typically have to be used close to the plants, within 2–4 inches of the leaves, to work well.

HID Lights

HID lights are called high-intensity discharge lights. They work by igniting and burning chemicals within them to produce massively bright lights. They come in two primary forms: metal halide (MH) lights and high-pressure sodium (HPS) lights. Each of these works slightly differently.

Generally, MH lights are recommended for stimulating leaves and stems into growing, while HPS lights are perfect for flowering. Keep in mind that these lights tend to produce significantly more heat than the other options, and you'll have to pay attention to this. In some cases, this may be beneficial, such as if you live somewhere that gets cold and you want to warm your tropical tree in the winter months. However, you may find that you need to set up some sort of ventilation to protect your plants and prevent them from burning. These lights also need to be kept further away, and you should do so at roughly 10 inches away.

LED Lights

While they were previously too expensive for many people to consider using, LED lights are actually highly effective. They've been slowly working their way into popularity because they are environmentally friendly, energy-efficient, and don't create much heat when they work. They are highly effective and customizable as well. You can swap them between several different spectrums, and you'll be able to use one light for several functions instead of having to constantly swap lights out. If you do choose to use these lights, keep in mind that you need to choose one that is reputable.

Lighting for Your Bonsai

Before you go out and set up a light, stop! What kind of bonsai do you have? Will it flower? What is its temperature tolerance level? You need to make sure you choose the right lights for your situation. It's recommended that you choose several lower-wattage lights rather than just one or two higher-wattage lights. This gives you more flexibility, especially because you are working with such small trees. You can add more bulbs if necessary, but if you have multiple bulbs, you can change the angles and the intensity of the light easier.

Your light should not be running 24/7. Make sure that you let your plants remain in the dark for between 6–12 hours per day to allow them to go dormant. Plants sleep and need time to rest, just like animals do. Just make sure that you don't suddenly shift your plant from outdoor to indoor, as the shift in light is likely to be problematic. Slowly introduce the light, maybe an hour at a time, working up to being indoors full time.

Propagation

Propagation refers to how plants reproduce. It can be done in two different ways: from a seed or from a cutting. Both of these allow a new plant to grow. The way that you chose to start your own tree is up to you, but you may find that you align closer with one of these methods than the other. Choose whichever works best for you.

Growing from Seed

Growing from seed is time-consuming but worth the effort. If you want to grow your bonsai tree from a seed, you first need to find a place where you can get the seed. You can either find them out in nature or purchase the specific kind of seed you want. Don't be fooled by labels claiming that they are specifically a "bonsai" seed. They may be part of a bonsai set, but bonsais are grown from normal seeds and will grow to normal proportions if you let them.

If you collect the seeds from your environment, they may need to be planted in the fall so they can go through stratification—a process by which the seeds are exposed to winter conditions so they can trigger germination and begin to grow.

If you buy online, make sure you do so from a trusted and reliable source, preferably from someone who is already familiar with bonsai trees. They will likely have healthy seeds that will translate into healthier plants as well.

BONSAI

When you have chosen your seed, it's time to start preparing for growing them.

1. **Preparing your seed:** Depending upon the species, they may not be ready to sprout immediately. Confirm whether you need to stratify the seed to get it ready to sprout. Many temperate species, such as maples, require this. During the cold and moist state, the tree can then prepare to germinate. If you're doing this at home or during an off-month, you can do the same thing by putting a seed in a baggy and filling it up with damp soil, then toss it into your fridge for three months. They should start to germinate, and you can plant them in the spring. Make sure you label the seeds you've used and write the number of seeds included. It's always better to over-plant than underplant. Choose to fill in many different plants and let them sit until they start to germinate. Whenever you see some sprouted seeds, remove them.

2. **Choosing soil:** After preparing the seeds, you'll need good soil. You can make the soil recommended, but it's generally a good idea to get organic potting soil and let your bonsai live in this for a few years before moving to the recommended soil discussed earlier.

3. **Filling the pot:** Next, fill up a pot with several holes to allow for drainage. Then, water the soil

to prepare it. Then, fill in the soil with several seeds to sprout.

4. **Caring for sproutlings:** Then, while the plants are growing, you can take care of them carefully. Some seeds will sprout in weeks, while others may take months. When they break out of their seeds, they'll start to grow quicker. You can move them to larger pots as necessary. Be mindful of removing them. You should do so by gently inserting a pencil underneath the roots and pushing them up instead of pulling by delicate stems.

Growing From Cuttings

You can also grow your new bonsai from a cutting. This process is known as cloning. You do so by taking a piece of another tree and encouraging it to sprout roots and grow as its own new tree. This is commonly done when a grower has a bonsai that they find to be desirable and they want to easily replicate the characteristics. They do so by cutting a piece and triggering the roots. This is typically much quicker than growing from seed and usually creates high-quality trees. Since you already know the genetics of the branch, you already know, more or less, what you're getting from the process. You've got one big benefit to this process: being able to grow multiple-trunked trees if you use a pronged branch. This can be highly desirable.

BONSAI

To do this, you really just have to take a piece of a tree and cultivate it in soil. After it roots, you can treat it like any other tree, and you'll be free to shape it to your whims.

- Cuttings are commonly either softwood, medium, or hardwood cuttings. These all offer slightly different benefits:

- **Softwood cuttings:** These cuttings are typically still green and fragile. You may have luck in this manner, but there's a chance that they won't take.

- **Medium cuttings:** These are typically taken in the fall, taking new growth from that year, but they've had the chance to become hard and woody at the trunk end, with the tip still green.

- **Hardwood cuttings:** These are from late fall or winter, and leaves have already fallen off. All vegetative growth has hardened.

The kind of cutting you choose is up to you. Generally, hardwood cuttings work well. Then, make sure you've got any rooting hormone necessary. This is a hormone that mimics the hormones that plants use to trigger root growth. If it's not a new bottle from the last few years, toss it out and get a new one *before* you start. Then, when you've got your rooting hormone ready, and you've chosen when you want to remove the cutting from a tree, you're ready to get started!

BONSAI

1. **Finding the right plant:** You begin by choosing the cutting you want to use and take the hormone with you. Then, if you're removing a cutting in the fall, you can remove the leaves with a sterile, sharp pair of scissors. Snip them all off just above the nodes.

2. **Separating the cutting from the tree:** When the leaves have been removed, identify a set of buds on the branch or twig. Then, snip it off right underneath the buds. Generally, you want to do this in increments of 5–7 inches to make the basis for your tree. Make sure your scissors or shears are sharp, so you don't damage the branch. After you cut, immerse them in water while you gather them.

3. **Rooting hormone:** After you've finished collecting potential cuttings to use, you can move on to the rooting hormone stage. You can either dip them into the powder or get the liquid form and apply them according to the instructions on the end that you want to root. Gently tap the cutting to remove any excess water or powder.

4. **Planting:** Once you've removed any excess hormone, you can then push a chopstick into a moist rooting medium to create a hole. Then, slip your cutting straight into the hole you created. This prevents you from accidentally removing the rooting hormone. Then, pat the medium down and into place. You can place several cuttings into

one large pot. Just make sure they are 1–2 inches apart from each other to give them plenty of space.

5. **Caring for your cuttings:** Hold off on watering right away as you want to make sure that your cuttings have the chance to absorb the hormone. Place the container in a safe place, in partial shade away from the wind. Let the medium dry out somewhat, and then water it again.

6. **Waiting for roots:** You'll know you're successful if you see new cuttings rooting in the spring. Make sure that the rooting medium is always moist to present damage to the new roots.

You can use just about anything for rooting containers and mediums, so long as they're appropriate. Root cuttings thrive in anything from river sand to coco peat and more. You just want to make sure that the medium can drain out better than loam or potting soil. Likewise, any container works, so long as you leave plenty of room for the drainage to occur. You don't want your plants getting too wet. Poking holes in yogurt containers are fair game here.

BONSAI

Chapter Summary

In this chapter, we covered the most important parts of cultivating your bonsai tree, including:

- Creating soil for your bonsai;
- Fertilizing your bonsai;
- Watering your bonsai;
- Providing ample light for your bonsai;
- Choosing the right sized container for your bonsai;
- Growing your bonsai from a seed;
- Growing your bonsai from a cutting;

In the next chapter, you will learn how you can get started with pruning and shaping your bonsai into any form you'd like.

BONSAI

CHAPTER EIGHT

PRUNING AND TRIMMING YOUR BONSAI

BONSAI

Once your bonsai is ready to be shaped, you'll probably be ecstatic! You've catered to it long enough that now, *finally*, you can start shaping it! It's a great day when a new bonsai is ready to be formed, but if you don't know what you're doing, you may struggle with knowing what you're doing. After all, too much trimming and pruning can be deadly to your plant. But, it's still good for you to know anyway; you need to have a solid understanding of how you can take care of your tree.

In this chapter, there are a few key considerations we're going to make. First, there's the deal with femininity and masculinity in regards to your tree. Before you start trimming it, you need to know whether you've got a masculine or feminine tree, so you know more or less how you want to shape it. From there, we'll delve into all essential aspects of pruning and trimming your bonsai so you can care for it to the best of your ability.

Keep in mind that the steps you're receiving here are more about how to take care of your tree. If you follow these steps, you will avoid damaging your tree. However, you'll already have to know how you plan on styling your tree. Think about the shape before you choose to do anything at all. Never start cutting if you don't have a solid idea of what to expect. Likewise, before you make any moves, make sure you double and triple-check the cuts.

Masculine vs. Feminine

Trees are typically classified as either masculine or feminine based upon the form the tree takes. This allows for an understanding of the pots' aesthetics as well. We'll be discussing masculine vs. feminine pots later, but for now, it's time to identify the way that you've chosen to form your tree. When you have a tree with matching aesthetics in the right pot, they're generally considered much nicer looking.

Feminine bonsais are known to be much more graceful. They're curvaceous and may have sparse foliage and thinner branches. They're typically more delicate-looking compared to masculine trees.

On the other hand, masculine trees are typically thicker and more upright. Generally, they also have more foliage and thicker ranches. If there is any use of deadwood or visible wounds, they're masculine in nature as well.

Of course, you don't have to know if your tree is a male or female; you just have to know how you want to style it. The choice you make will then determine how you prune or trim your tree, and later, will influence how you choose to wire your tree when we get to the next chapter.

Pruning Your Bonsai

You might think that pruning is as simple as snipping off a few branches, but there's so much more to it. You need to know which branches need to be cut and which should be allowed to continue growing. You'll need to make sure that you take care and thought to figure out which branches need to go so you can turn your tree into a beautiful piece of living art.

Why Bonsais Need Pruning

Typically, pruning has two key purposes: One is to ensure that your tree is healthy. The second is to ensure that your tree is aesthetic. You are combining art with health, and remember that beauty will be what you define it as. What matters is that your tree is what you want.

Before you prune, try sketching a plan of what you want your tree to look like eventually. You'll need to be able to see what your tree should look like when you're done so you can work on getting to that point as easily as possible. When you know what the final goal is, you'll be able to tell if you need to let something keep growing or if you need to remove it. You'll be trying to eventually maintain the final design for several years after the fact, but sometimes, you have to let some branches grow out first.

Structural Pruning

Structural pruning comes first. This is the kind of pruning you do to train a young bonsai into the form you want to see. You usually do so more intensely than you'd normally trim because you remove primary branches in order to get the eventual aesthetic you're looking for.

Typically, the bottom-most branches are removed first. This is good for the tree's health, as the bottom branches will be a drain on nutrients.

After the bottom branches go, you want to remove all of the unhealthy branches as well. You want to find anything that's weak, yellowing, or otherwise damaged.

Cross branches are typically removed as well, as they're not aesthetic. These are branches that will cross over other branches.

Branches that grow up or down are usually taken off due to a lack of aesthetics.

In traditional Japanese bonsai, branches that grow forward, as in toward the viewer, are typically removed as well. Pointing is considered rude in Japan, so any branches pointing directly at the viewer are also considered rude.

These pruning cuts are all considered structural. They are supposed to help create the right look for the tree. These cuts can be quite draining for the tree, so you'll want to do so in either spring or fall, so your tree has a chance to heal.

Maintenance Pruning

This kind of pruning is more about ensuring that you keep the design of your tree intact. It includes several different actions, such as leaf and twig pruning and pinching. It serves two purposes. Removing leaves where they've grown too thick allows your tree to get more air and light and to remain healthier. You get to keep the tree's natural aesthetic as well. Ideally, maintenance pruning should occur from mid-March to September.

BONSAI

Deciduous trees will require leaf pruning sometimes. A trick to knowing which leaves to prune is to find leaves in pairs and take one per pair off.

- **Defoliation:** This is the removal of leaves from a bonsai. Some people will remove all leaves in the summertime in order to encourage smaller leaves to grow. To do so, you remove the leaf while leaving the leaf stem in place. As a beginner, you probably shouldn't remove more than a third of the leaves at any given time. You also have to make sure that you only do this to a plant that has not recently been heavily pruned or repotted.

- **Bud Pinching:** All pines and some conifers will require you to pinch buds. This is to remove some of the needles from the tree to maintain the aesthetic you're looking for. You can do so by pinching certain leaves between the thumb and forefinger and then twisting and pulling.

How to Prune Your Bonsai Tree

Pruning your bonsai isn't a difficult task. In just six steps, you'll be able to manage your trees well.

Step 1: Gather Tools

The first step is to gather up your tools. You'll need to use shears and concave cutters primarily. They need to be sharp, so they will cut through without causing damage to the branches. Make sure they're of suitable sizes for the branches you'll be trimming.

Step 2: Determine Cuts

The second step is to determine where you need to cut. Start with your tree on a flat surface, preferably at eye level. Take the time to look at the tree to determine where you believe you'll need to trim, keeping in mind that imperfection is acceptable. You're looking for balance, and that doesn't mean that you need it to be perfect. There is a beauty in imperfection, and in traditional Japanese aesthetics, the concept of wabi-sabi must be remembered. This is the view that accepts transience and imperfection. When you accept the imperfections, you accept the beauty in nature, which is imperfect, impermanent, and incomplete. Plan your tree with this in mind.

Step 3: Deadwood

The third step is to look for the deadwood around the bonsai. Remove it where you can find it. Some artists may preserve and accentuate the look, but managing deadwood is difficult in most cases and isn't recommended for beginners.

Step 4: Pruning

Fourth, you need to start the pruning process. If you're using structural pruning, make clean cuts as you do so. For maintenance pruning, remember to assess regularly during the process.

BONSAI

Step 5: Prepping Branches

The fifth step is to prep any branches. You want to apply healing paste to them to keep them from healing poorly or developing some sort of infection.

After Pruning Care

When you finish pruning your tree, the next step is to water it well. Your tree will need plenty of water to heal.

BONSAI

Chapter Summary

In this chapter, we've gone over some important aspects of pruning your tree.

- You need to know when to prune the specific species of tree that you have before getting started.

- Wabi-sabi matters, and your tree doesn't have to be perfect. It just has to be balanced.

- Remember to provide your tree with plenty of water after it's been pruned.

Next, we will address how to wire your tree to ensure you get the perfect shape the way you want it.

BONSAI

CHAPTER NINE

WIRING YOUR BONSAI

BONSAI

We tend to associate bonsais with that bent look that is created primarily through wiring and clipping in order to shape them. There's an art to creating the perfect picture when it comes to your bonsai, and the sooner you learn how to do so, the better.

As you read through this chapter, we've got a few key points to go over that are essential to your ability to create your own bonsai. These include the benefits of wiring, how to choose the wire, when you should wire, how to wire, and how to remove the wire when you're done shaping your tree. As you go over everything, you'll learn what you need to do from start to finish. However, before you get started, keep in mind that some trees don't tolerate wiring as much, as we've already mentioned. Do a bit of research on the specific species before you commit to anything to guarantee that you aren't inadvertently hurting your tree.

Benefits of Bonsai Wiring

Wiring serves two key benefits to bonsai as they grow. First, it serves as a way that you can mold your tree. You can't force a tree to take a form that you want without intervening somehow, and it isn't going to magically take on the form you want it to just because you wish for it really hard. However, what you can do is wire it to coax it into that position over time, even if the position appears to be quite unnatural.

Additionally, it also creates a boost to the aesthetic of the tree. Yes, you can generally shape your tree with pruning to an extent, but wiring makes the impossible suddenly possible as well, and you can use that to your advantage.

Choosing Wire

Before you begin, choose which kind of wire you prefer to use. Your primary options are either copper or aluminum wires. Sometimes, this is just a matter of opinion, but other times, it's a good idea to use one wire over the other. No matter what kind of wire you're using, there's a general rule that will help you select the right size. Any wire should be roughly a third of the diameter of the branch that you're wiring.

Copper wire is typically stronger than aluminum. This allows it to hold its place better when you place it somewhere. This is sometimes useful when working with harder wood or stubborn trees. However, it comes with its own drawbacks as well. Copper wire is not very forgiving, and it can potentially cut into the plant if you're not watching carefully. If you're not careful, you could unintentionally cut into the trees simply because you didn't loosen the wire as the tree was growing.

Aluminum wire is usually the recommended choice for beginners because it isn't as likely to cut into quickly growing branches. It is not as strong, but you'll be able to adjust it regularly and keep your plant shaping normally. Aluminum is also easier to manipulate in general. You'll be able to look at it every other week instead of every week, as is the case with copper.

When to Wire

It can be tough to know when to start wiring your tree, but this depends mostly on whether you're writing a deciduous or coniferous tree. Each has different growing cycles that you'll need to consider. Trees grow differently depending on the species, making a big difference in how you grow and shape them.

Deciduous trees do best when you wire in early spring, typically before any new budding begins. When you wire at this time, you have a better view of the trunk and branches before the new leaves start growing. You'll also get the chance to wire without any new leaves and branches impeding you.

You will want to wire coniferous trees in either late fall or early winter. This is because these trees will renew foliage cyclically, so their limbs will always have some. Instead of worrying about visual fields, you worry about when the sap is at the lowest in the branches. Typically, during the late fall or winter season, the sap is at its lowest, and the branches are bound to be more flexible.

Make sure that when you do wire, you don't choose to wire any weak, unhealthy branches. If you wire a weak plant, it may not be able to tolerate the stress. Weak branches are unlikely to be able to hold against the strain. Spend some time nurturing the tree back up to better health before wiring. You also don't want to wire a plant that has been freshly watered because the branches are more likely to be flexible when dehydrated somewhat.

How to Wire

When it's time to wire, you need to ensure that you've chosen the right plant, the right time, and the right wire. Then, you'll simply carefully wrap the branch with wire. However, it's not about just wrapping. You need to support the plant during the process, holding the limb with both hands. Remember that you are bending your wire onto the branch instead of forcing the branch to bend to the wire.

Start at the trunk and work your way up from thicker branches to thinner ones. Bend them so they move up the trunk and out instead of in any other position, and you should always be wiring in the direction toward you instead of the other way around.

As you wire, wrap it at a 45-degree angle. The wire should then guide the direction without being tight enough to constrict it. You need to account for the fact that it will be growing while you are applying the wire, and if you're not careful, what you'll end up with is a wire that cuts straight into the tree as it grows, scarring the branch.

After wiring, you can provide anchoring to prevent crossed wires or excess tension. The wire should start with a firm foundation in the soil and should feel steady. Then, wire the trunk. Start with a tight angle where the wire comes from the ground, then focus on keeping the wire support at the 45-degree angle.

BONSAI

Remember that the thickness of the wire matters. You can use the same piece of wire on several branches if they're the same size, but otherwise, don't. Make it a point to change to the right-sized wire each time you need to. If you're dealing with a tougher, stronger branch, you can even choose to use several strands of wire together to create additional support.

Removing the Wire

Eventually, the wire will have achieved its purpose or will no longer be large enough. As the plant begins to grow, if the wire is kept too tightly, it's going to cause damage. When it's time to remove the wire, you can do so by using a pair of wire cutters. It might be tempting to unwind the wire from the tree so you can reuse it, but don't do this. You could damage or break the branch, which would set you back considerably. It's better to take your time and snip off the excess wires slowly. You can easily buy more wire, but you'd lose years and years if you damaged the bonsai. It's always better to put the tree first.

BONSAI

Chapter Summary

In this chapter, we went over how to wire a tree to mold it into the proper shape for whatever you wanted for your tree.

- Aluminum wire is recommended for beginners.
  - The wire should always be a third of the thickness of the diameter of the branch you're attempting to mold.
  - Check wire regularly to make sure it doesn't dig into the branch.

In the next chapter, we will address the ins and outs of repotting your bonsai. This is an essential tool that you'll likely need every few years.

BONSAI

CHAPTER TEN

REPOTTING

BONSAI

Bonsais require repotting sometimes, but your plants probably aren't going to be very happy about it. When you repot your bonsai, you are going to remove it from one pot to move it to another. However, it's not quite as simple as moving from one pot to the next. You're going to need to do some general maintenance during this time to ensure that your plant stays comfortable and healthy.

Repotting is perhaps one of the most important parts of taking care of your bonsai. And yet, it's the one that beginners get wrong the most. There's a lot of bad information about how to repot, and failing to do so well can be catastrophic if you haven't been taking care of your plant well. To master the process, you're going to need to pay attention to your tree and learn how to take care of it carefully.

In this chapter, we will go over what repotting is, why it's essential, when to do it, and how to ensure it's done well. We'll also address how to prune the roots and how you can nurse your tree back to health after you've repotted it. These are all essential skills that will need to happen if you want to keep your tree happy and healthy.

What is Repotting?

Repotting your tree is the process of taking your tree and putting it in a new pot. It may involve root pruning if necessary, and it happens to keep your plants healthy. You do this because the tree is kept in a very small container. While the tree is in this small container, the entire container can fill up with roots, at which point the plant will start to suffer. Prevent this by repotting the tree. You remove it from the previous pot and trim the roots before placing it back into its pot with fresh soil, or potentially a larger pot if you need to move up.

Why Repot the Bonsai?

Your plant's roots are essential to its livelihood. Without healthy roots, the bonsai will not be able to take in what it needs. It won't be able to get its water or minerals from the ground to continue growing well. It will also run out of space to absorb oxygen, which plants need to take in from the roots as well.

Soil is filled with all sorts of natural holes and gaps within it that trees penetrate in order to grow. As those pockets of air start to fill in with roots, the soil's porosity goes down as well. As a result, the roots are slowly kept from growing. As they struggle to grow and lose out on oxygen, the end result is delayed growth in the leaves.

When you have plants like bonsais in small containers, they can suffer from this much quicker. Bonsais get relatively little soil, which they can quickly overfill and run out of oxygen. This is where repotting comes into play. Regular repotting will replenish the soil's porosity. Trim back the roots where you can so they won't fail. If you were never to repot or prune the roots, you would wind up eventually killing the tree.

BONSAI

When to Repot

Repotting may need to happen annually, or sometimes five to ten years apart. The timing is all about knowing the tree you need. You'll need to look for signs that your plant needs repotting so you can protect your tree. Consider looking for these signs to know when to repot.

- When soil grows compact, the tree may struggle to get enough water. It could help to slow the growth and reduce the internode length, which may age the look of the bonsai, but you may struggle to grow it.

- A slower growth rate compared to previous seasons may indicate a need to repot.

- Soil doesn't absorb water readily.

- Reduced uptake of water in summer months.

- Leaf size is reducing.

- Leaf drop occurs in early fall.

- Foliage starts to yellow or become less glossy.

- Fine twigging dies in the winter.

- Slime growing on the surface of the soil.

- The root ball is rising out of the pot.

BONSAI

- Leaves drop after a few weeks of growing.

Most of the time, you'll want to repot your deciduous trees right as the buds of the leaves start opening up. Evergreens usually prefer to be repotted just as their own buds start unfurling as well. When you repot too early, you can actually impair the growth of the trees. Some tropical species prefer to be repotted mid-summer instead. Some pines also prefer to repot after they've stopped their annual growth.

Root Pruning

Root pruning is the process of trimming the roots down when necessary to prevent them from overgrowing. Roots are essential, taking in the water and minerals that the plant needs, but they also serve as an anchor. Without this anchor, the tree wouldn't be able to support itself.

Roots grow underground and push themselves through the soil. As they do, the tip of the root is usually capped to prevent damage. The white roots are not yet woody; they're usually softer and easily damaged. After a few weeks, they become woody as well, becoming anchors for the tree.

Root pruning prevents the roots from continuing to extend. When pruned properly, the tree will develop new white feeder roots from where the lignified roots were cut. This creates a stronger tree as well. You're improving efficiency. With a smaller but more robust root system, your tree expends less energy trying to grow outward.

BONSAI

There is no need to support the old, lignified roots that won't provide many benefits anyway since there's no need to push them through soil that isn't there in the first place.

If the roots were left to grow endlessly, there is a chance that it would take far longer for the nutrients and water to make their way through the roots to the main tree, and the tree may even eventually starve. This is where root pruning comes into play. Follow a few steps to prune your roots.

1. Take the tree out from the growing container and set it somewhere you can work. Gently comb through the roots using your fingers or a root comb so that you can remove loose soil or roots.

2. Trim the roots circling the main taproot.

3. Shorten thicker storage roots that grow downward from the taproot, taking off roughly a third of their length and leaving behind the hair roots.

4. Cut ⅓ of the lower portion of root structures with pruning clippers.

5. Select a container that is roughly 1 inch taller than the root ball after you've pruned it and replant it.

How to Repot

Repotting isn't too difficult if you know what you're doing. Start by withholding water for a few days. This is

BONSAI

because repotting when you have very wet soil is going to be difficult. It will be much easier with dryer soil, so you don't make a big mess. Mud can make it difficult to see where you should be making your cuts. Then, when you're certain you have everything on hand, including a new suitable pot if necessary, soil to fill it, and mesh to prevent anything from sliding through the drainage holes.

Remove the tree from the previous pot and begin to rake out the soil. Follow the steps involved in root pruning from here on out if you intend to do so. You may face a thick, knotted root ball, but working through it is still your best bet. The most important thing to remember is that you want to remove enough of the soil that the root ball cannot become solid.

When you have clean roots that have been pruned, you can then return the tree to a pot. Ensure the drainage holes have plastic mesh held in place with aluminum wire. Then, pass some aluminum wire through the drainage hole going up toward the tree. Typically, you'll want 2 mm for smaller trees or up to 4 mm for larger trees to secure it into place.

Put some of the new soil into the pot so the tree can stand on it. Pass the wire over some of the heavy roots and twist so you can leave the tree standing on its own. Then, add a bit of soil at a time, making sure it gets between the roots. Gently use a chopstick to fill in gaps. Fill all the cavities and settle the pot with the right amount of soil. Then, secure the wire around the base of the roots with pliers. Then, press it into the base.

BONSAI

Water the tree well after you've planted it until the pot floods and water continues to pass through. If you're using akadama, continue to water until it's clear as it comes out of the drainage holes.

BONSAI

Chapter Summary

In this chapter, we went over the importance of being able to repot your plant properly. Being able to repot it well may make the difference between a healthy and unhealthy plant.

- Pruning older roots is essential to keeping good health. It does not hurt the tree at all.

- Repotting is necessary every few years or so to keep your tree healthy.

- Watering is essential aftercare to help your plant to survive the process of root trimming.

The next chapter will focus on any necessary seasonal care your tree may require to keep healthy. Trees evolved to be outside, so they expect to go through all of the seasons, especially if you've chosen a species that is not native near the equator.

BONSAI

CHAPTER ELEVEN

SEASONAL CARE

BONSAI

Winter weather is a threat to bonsais everywhere, especially because the root systems of bonsais are so shallow. In nature, trees have roots that go so deeply below the ground that they rarely suffer from freezing temperatures. The first few inches may freeze, but the rest is kept warm enough to protect the trees. However, your bonsai doesn't get the same luxury. Your bonsai is going to be exposed to the winter conditions because its roots are so vulnerable. If you're growing your bonsai outdoors in the winter, you'll need to do something that will protect the vulnerable roots as much as you can if you want to keep them alive.

The top of trees tends to get hit with the full brunt of winter chills and is usually designed to live through it, so long as you've chosen a species that is native to your area or climate. Tropical plants may not tolerate winter conditions if you live somewhere cold, but many species should do well, even with moderately freezing temperatures, if taken care of properly.

Some trees will require more specific overwintering criteria than others, so do your due diligence before prepping your bonsai for winter. You will need to pay attention to the specific needs of whichever trees you have if you want to ensure that they stay healthy.

Fall Care

In the fall, it's normal for most temperate deciduous trees to lose their foliage in preparation for dormancy. Some species, such as boxwoods, may maintain the same foliage for several years, but otherwise, more often than not, you'll notice the leaves change colors and die off before falling down. Evergreens won't lose foliage, but the color may change somewhat during this period as well.

There is some care that you'll need to remember in the fall to prepare your trees for survival in the winter. With a few simple changes to how you take care of your tree, you can prepare it to survive the winter readily.

The first thing to remember is that tropical plants probably need to start making their way indoors as the days start getting shorter. Tropical plants will not survive if the temperatures drop too low, so you may need to help them stay alive.

You will want to keep a few things in mind for your deciduous and evergreen trees during fall.

Enough Sunlight for the Trees

As the fall weather comes in, the sun is no longer right overhead. This means that the positions that you kept your trees during the summer may no longer yield enough sunlight for them to thrive. This means that you're going to need to provide them with sunlight in other ways. Move them to other places to get more sunlight. This is especially the case if you have junipers and pines that require lots of time in the sunlight. Deciduous trees will be preparing to shed their leaves at this point and won't really need the same amount of sunlight as the evergreens, so prioritize getting enough sunlight for the evergreens.

BONSAI

Adjust the Watering Schedule

As fall comes, you may need to adjust the watering schedule. It's cold, and it might rain a lot, but you'll also want to keep in mind that even if it rains, your trees won't be getting enough water. You'll still want to regularly check whether or not your trees need water before making any assumptions. The containers are also quite small, so it's unlikely that even rain will give enough water to them directly into the soil. Foliage may block it, or there may just not be enough falling to gather enough in such a short period.

Fertilize

At this time of the year, you need to provide your plants with a burst of fertilization. Providing your plants with fertilizer in the fall ensures that they're ready to start growing in the spring. Make sure that you choose an organic fertilizer and apply it regularly during this period.

Double-Check the Drainage of your Tree's Pot

Early spring brings the time to start repotting, so now's the time to start looking for signs of whether this is going to have to happen. Check to make sure that water still runs freely in the pots. If it does, then you're probably fine to skip repotting. However, if you notice that the water isn't draining effectively, you may need to repot immediately.

When there's no room for the water to clear out, then you've got a new problem on your hands: root rot

BONSAI

and a lack of oxygen. Or, if that remains the case into the winter, you may even turn your root ball into an ice cube, which your tree will not appreciate.

Make sure there's nothing blocking the drainage mesh, including slugs that may want to make their homes there. If nothing is blocking it, then the next step is probably an emergency repotting to ensure that your plant won't accidentally drown during this time. If you're repotting, skip the root trimming if you can.

Final Pruning and Wiring for the Year

As the leaves start to change color, it's a good idea to start your final pruning season. Of course, you'll want to ensure that the cuts are sealed properly to prevent sap loss and to encourage healing. Since the tree's leaves are dying during this time, there's no harm in removing the leaves. Once you know that there are no more buds coming, you're free to work with the plant during this time. You can wire without concern for buds. You can also see how the outline of your tree is coming into place during this time. Take the time to understand where you need to trim your tree and be mindful of where you put the wires as well to help create the vision you're intending. If you do wire during the fall, make sure that you do so and pay close attention to when the tree starts growing again come spring, or you could unintentionally damage it.

BONSAI

Winter Care

You might be tempted to think that your bonsai will be fine indoors in the winter without anything special, but that's not necessarily the case! Some may be fine to do so, but others may require a long period of dormancy in the winter to grow healthily. If you can't provide that, your plants are going to struggle more.

Being able to take care of your bonsai in the wintertime is essential—you don't want to kill it unintentionally. So, what are you to do? Simple. There are many ways that you can work on taking care of your plant. Before you start that, however, keep in mind that there are different hardiness levels.

Tropical bonsais cannot tolerate freezing at all. They must be kept indoors in the winter if your temperatures drop low. Semi-tropical bonsais can tolerate mild to moderate frost in the short term but will not do well if the temperatures stay low for too long. Temperate bonsais are capable of withstanding frozen temperatures without any damage at all. Finally, hard bonsai can take on extreme cold for long periods without damage.

Regardless of the type of bonsai, there are ways that you can protect your tree from freezing. For example, you can cover your tree with a cloth and then a piece of plastic over the cloth. This will allow for more warmth. The plastic will help promote the heat overnight. Then, as the sun rises, remove the cloth and plastic so the leaves can breathe.

BONSAI

You also must make sure that you know whether your plant should be indoors or outdoors at any given point during the winter. Some trees want to be outdoors, while others may appreciate the interior shelter. Check with the specific species you've chosen before doing anything at all.

When you grow your plants outdoors, make sure you prevent the soil from drying out still. You might not have to add much water to it but do so if you notice it gets dry. Your tree won't need much moisture during dormancy. Some people also like to plant their trees directly into the soil during the winter months to protect them. The soil will help insulate, and because there's more of it, the plant will stay warmer. If you can't do this, you could use a wooden pot filled up with soil and plant your bonsai in this instead. The more soil you have, the more you can trust your plant to be insulated.

Dormancy and Your Bonsai

As winter arrives, normally, trees will enter dormancy. This is how they prevent themselves from being damaged by the cold of winter, which would otherwise wreak havoc on their systems. They slowly shut down and wait until the spring warmth triggers the development of leaf buds and other new growth.

While you might think that your trees will die outside, this is not necessarily the case. If anything, exposing them to the temperatures and lights that you'd have indoors may actually harm your tree. The internal clock of your tree requires a period of dormancy, much in the way that when you fly on a plane around the world, you stay on the same sleep schedule that you were on before. The shift in the daytime and nighttime throws off your circadian rhythm, and, in the same way, pulling your tree inside for the winter will confuse it as well. The tree may continue to grow inside after pulling it in, but eventually, the tree will not be able to fight it off anymore. Leaves will drop off, and evergreens will stop growing. If the plant is out of season during this dormancy period that happens, it may even die as a result.

Trees will require different amounts of dormancy. If you live where the winter is mild, dormancy may be difficult to trigger naturally. However, your tree will need it if it is a species that originates from an area with mild winters. This is where putting your tree into dormancy will come into play. You may need to force the point in order to get it to rest. You can do this in a dark garage or put your plant in a refrigerator. Your tree will require, at the bare minimum, 11 to 42 days of constant temperatures below 50 °F to keep it alive and well.

Preparing for the Winter

It's a good idea to start preparing for your tree's dormancy before winter comes. From May to November, try to allow your bonsai to be outdoors as much as possible for optimum sunlight. The natural sunlight also prepares the tree as the cycles of light change.

You should also slow down dramatically with the fertilization come late August, and avoid doing any pruning before winter because your tree will spend a lot of resources trying to heal, which can leave it vulnerable to the winter. Do all pruning two months before winter or in the spring.

During Winter Care

When you're in the dormancy period, it's recommended that you allow your trees to rest somewhere cool, dark, and unheated, especially if you live in a cold climate. If you have a hardy species, it may be fine on its own outdoors regardless of the weather.

If you keep your tree indoors in the winter, it won't need light so long as the temperature is between 20 and 50 °F. As it experiences the early cold temperatures, it will trigger the tree to prepare for winter.

If you can't leave your tree outside, you can also refrigerate it during its dormant period and then move it indoors in late winter to begin preparing. However, if you do this, make sure that the temperature is between 35 and 40 °F.

After Winter Care

When the cold has passed, you can repot your bonsai. You'll want to do this before the spring growth period, as you don't want your plant to get too big and needing to be pruned back significantly during this time.

What About Tropical and Subtropical Bonsais?

BONSAI

If you have a tropical or subtropical species, dormancy is actually not needed. In fact, these trees may even suffer and die if you try to leave them outdoors in the winter. Tropical and subtropical trees are required to be indoors during fall, winter, and spring. These trees will require you to keep them indoors regularly. You'll need to ensure that they are kept safe from harm in other ways instead.

Tropical and subtropical trees are typically capable of growing all year round, so long as the weather is warmer. This makes them suitable for indoor bonsais, and you can even let them enjoy the outdoors more during the summer, so they aren't indoors all the time. Growing them outside in the summer means they often get the more intense light they usually like while still getting to stay indoors.

BONSAI

Chapter Summary

During this chapter, we went over the most important care for winter, as well as preparing in the fall to ensure that the overwintering process is a success.

- Start in the fall to prepare your plant to survive wintering.

- Make sure all tropical and subtropical plants come indoors.

- Ensure that your pot is draining well so it will drain all winter.

In the next chapter, you will learn about how to show off your bonsai.

BONSAI

CHAPTER TWELVE

SHOWING OFF YOUR BONSAI

BONSAI

And finally, as we wrap up the book, we're going to consider the effort that goes into being able to show off your bonsai. Your tree is a piece of art that deserves to be honored and displayed beautifully. And, in traditional bonsai, people select the perfect pots to balance out and ensure that everything looks good. The best bonsai are those that show the harmony and joining of the design of the tree alongside the beauty of the container.

In this chapter, we'll address several key components. First, we'll consider the basics of bonsai display. Then, we'll go into how to determine the perfect container for your tree, going over everything that usually determines the kind of container you should get. With this information, you should be able to piece together exactly what you'll need to create a successful tree that is beautiful and worth showing off to everyone around you.

The Basics of Bonsai Display

The entire purpose of your bonsai tree is to be seen. The work that you go into it is just one part of the whole; if it isn't displayed well, it can never be appreciated to the fullest extent that it deserves. Displaying bonsai isn't supposed to be difficult or complex. You might need to consider many aspects, but ultimately, there are just three major points that will help you.

The Bonsai is the Center

The center of your display will always be the bonsai. You need to set the bonsai up with the right support, but ultimately, no matter how beautiful the support and display are, an ugly bonsai will bring the whole thing down. As you design your bonsai, remember the essential aspects, such as ensuring that you've got balance within the tree while still honoring the concept of wabi-sabi, will matter the most. You need to ensure that your tree will be well put together if you want it to be enjoyed by others.

Bonsai Displays Create Harmony

You also want to consider harmony. Your bonsai is just one part of a greater whole. You also need to consider the other aspects that go into it. The display should be all about balancing and invoking that sense of nature.

Everything Should Be Intentional

Finally, remember that every aspect, from the color of the pot to how the whole tree looks, should be one beautiful, harmonious piece that works well together and should be planned out. When you manage this, you'll find that you have much greater success. Everything that you do should be perfect.

The Elements of a Bonsai Display

Before you get started, you'll need to understand the various elements and objects that you'll use to put your bonsai display together. Ensuring proper harmony is going to make your display much more effective. You're going to want to pay attention to how these objects all work together. Typically, the goal is to create an asymmetrical triangle with a dimension that is also in a cohesive scene.

BONSAI

Companion Objects

Typically, bonsai displays include what is called a companion object. These are other elements or objects beyond the plant, the pot, and the stand that are meant to enhance the look. When these companion objects are in place, you can get a much better look. Most commonly, you may see the following included:

- Scrolls
- Suiseki (mountain stones)

BONSAI

- Floral plants that are much smaller than the bonsai

- A small statue with a natural element depicted

Choosing a companion object is all about selecting items that come together with your bonsai. There's no real rule to this, so long as you select something that contributes to the scene. Let your heart and nature be the guide. If you want to display your bonsai with a plant or statue of an animal, make sure they are animals or plants that would occur naturally in the wild with your bonsai.

If you choose something like scrolls, you may want to select something subtle. Something with a natural element in harmony with your bonsai would be a good idea. You can select up to two objects, but try to aim for one. You're not trying to compete with the bonsai.

Pot

The pot is another essential object that you'll need to consider early on. The color must be harmonious with the bonsai, and it should be the right size as well. It should appear to be a natural extension from the width of the bonsai. We've already gone into how to determine the right size of a pot, and shortly, we'll dive in-depth into how to select the perfect container.

The Stand

You'll also want to have a good stand for your bonsai. Called "shoku" in Japan, these stands are meant to

BONSAI

be at eye level to ensure people get to look straight at the display. The stand should be the right size, without being so ornamental that they're distracting from the main bonsai. Typically, darker woods are traditional for most bonsai, but if you have a flowering bonsai, you may prefer a lighter wood.

Placing the Display

The placement of your display is essential. Nothing should be an afterthought, including where you put your bonsai. It should ideally be somewhere that is centered while providing three sides from which your display will be viewable. It's okay for it to be against a wall, but make sure that people can view from either side as well as the front. Your background should be somewhere soft and neutral, but not white, as this is too bright and harsh. You want to find a softer color, perhaps a tan or beige, that won't compete. The whole display should be well-lit, so your plant will receive enough lighting and is in a meaningful area.

Once you've chosen a place for the display, it's time to figure out where you want to put the rest of the objects on top of it. Remember that you're trying to create a harmonious display that has perspective and dimension.

Placing the Bonsai

Typically, you will have an asymmetrical triangle for your display. You usually want to place your bonsai on the opposite side of its pull. For example, if your bonsai leans

BONSAI

left, make sure you place it more to the right on the display. The end of the tree is usually centered on the stand, while the trunk and pot are to the side.

Placing the Companion Objects

When you place your companion object, do so on the opposite side of the pot, away from the bonsai. It should be as far away from the nearest sidewall as the bonsai is from its nearest sidewall, but you need to shift the horizontal axis. Place it either closer or further away from the front of the display to create dimension to the triangle.

If you've chosen stones, they usually represent mountains, and as such, they have to be placed closer to the back wall, creating a sense of distance. Flowering plants and statues are usually placed closer to the viewer.

Choosing the Perfect Container

The perfect container can be difficult to pull off if you don't know what you're doing, but you'll need to have one to bring the entire image together. It is not easy, and in some cases, can even be as hard as picking out the tree itself. There are many different pot designs, colors, glazes, and more, making this a very difficult process, and yet it's one that you'll need to figure out for yourself.

This is one of the most important aspects, but it's also something that is highly subjective. You'll need to keep your personal tastes in mind as well. Some may prefer something more traditional and conservative, while others prefer more colorful containers. You'll need to consider dimensions, as discussed earlier. However, when selecting your pot, you want to be able to look at shape, color, and texture.

Masculine vs. Feminine Pots

We often assign a gender to our trees when we create a design. It isn't required, but it is a common aspect. Masculine trees are supposed to evoke feelings of strength. Feminine trees, on the other hand, tend to be more delicate and smooth.

Certain trees are more predisposed to being masculine or feminine. Pines and hawthorns tend to be masculine, and Japanese maples tend to be feminine. Strong, angular branches will be deemed masculine while flowing, lithe branches appear to be feminine.

The gender of your tree matters because they can be matched with pots. Pots are also typically considered masculine and feminine and you'll need to select the right ones for your tree.

As a general rule, masculine pots are typically deeper, with stronger angles. These may be strong, with rectangular shapes and sharp corners. They may also be square and deeply set. They are well-suited for masculine trees as a result. Feminine pots, on the other hand, are usually less deep and rounded in shape. They're usually delicate ovals or even literati pots.

BONSAI

Pot Shape

The shape you choose is widely dependent upon the tree you've selected. Typically, coniferous species or larger deciduous trees with a lot of tapers and heavy nebari are quite masculine. These belong in a larger, rectangular pot.

On the other hand, if you have a deciduous tree that is quite feminine and clumps, and is very curvy, you'll want to consider an oval pot.

Rounded pots are suitable for either coniferous or feminine trees. This is especially true for literati or other curvy trees. Tall and straight or trees with little taper tend to be best-suited to shallow round pots.

Pot Rim

The rim of your tree also matters in creating the intended look. A lip on the upper rim adds strength and is considered more masculine. A straight rim is considered to be softer and is for more neutral androgynous trees. Feminine trees do best with bowls or convex sides.

Pot Feet

Feet on bonsai pots is usually a good idea so you can get good drainage while also encouraging airflow. However, they may also change the display of the pot dramatically. They could be subtle, or they could be strong. Typically, bigger, stronger feet will create a stronger, masculine look while delicate or understated feet appear feminine.

Pot Corners

The corners also matter. Of course, masculine pots are those shaped in squares and rectangles, so here, we're predominantly considering masculine trees. Indented corners may soften the masculinity somewhat. Sharp corners are considered highly masculine and very strong. Rounding out corners to soften the pot, but not so much that it is an oval, is suitable for masculine deciduous trees.

Pot Colors

Once you've chosen the right shape for your pot, it's time to consider the right color as well. When you are choosing the right color, you will need to consider the tree itself. Every tree is unique, and two trees, even of the same species, are not the same. This is why there's no real way to generalize a color to each species. However, there are some standard rules you can use to narrow it down.

The pot's color will help to pick up on something about the tree in the best situations and help create cohesion between the two. Maybe you choose to complement the color of the bark or the fruit or leaves. It may only show signs of matching for part of the year. No matter what, however, remember that this is a personal choice. If you've got a thought on something that is atypical, that doesn't mean that it's wrong. If you choose an unconventional pot, that's because you have chosen to, and that's okay, so long as it is an intentional choice on your end.

BONSAI

Generally speaking, the following colors tend to suit themselves to the following trees:

- **Dark green:** Azalea, Japanese maple, cotoneaster, Chinese elm

- **Grey and off-white:** Japanese maple, oak, hawthorn, ash

- **Light blue:** Flowering species

- **Light brown or oatmeal:** Japanese maple, elm, beech, larch, ash, gingko, oak,

- **Light green:** Beech, ash, Japanese maple

- **Matte blue:** Azalea, pine, juniper, Japanese maple

- **Matte green:** Azalea, Japanese maple, juniper, pine

- **Medium Brown:** Japanese maple, mountain ash, birch, elm

- **Red-brown, unglazed red, or brown:** Juniper, pine, azalea, larch, cotoneaster, conifers

Of course, this isn't a hard rule. You may see something unconventional that works quite well, and that's okay too. It's all about bringing out your most personal, authentic self with whatever that may be.

Pot Textures

Finally, the texture of your pot will matter as well. If you look closely at pots, you'll notice that some appear to be perfectly smooth while others may have a grittier, rugged look to them. This variation allows for even more personalization for your bonsai. If you want a beautiful, cohesive look, one way to do so is by choosing the right texture.

Generally speaking, the more feminine trees get smoother clay finishes when compared to masculine pots. Masculine pots tend to be much more heavily textured. This is because they are supposed to appear to be wild and more masculine as a result.

These may pair with the color in several ways. A pot that is highly textured and very gritty or coarse may be well-suited to a pine, especially when using a matte blue or green glaze over it.

Some pots may also have texture developed within the glaze, creating softer, more subtle textures when compared to the pots used for masculine trees. Others may be perfectly smoothed out, perfect for feminine pots.

Ultimately, choosing a pot is not easy by any means. It's a combination of knowing how different elements come together while then bringing your experience and knowledge into it. Choosing the right pot is something that you have to decide for yourself for it to be highly

BONSAI

successful. If you know what you're doing, you should find that you can make great progress.

When you buy your pot, don't forget to consider the measurements that you'll need. The last thing you want to do is pick up the wrong option because you weren't really paying attention, and you discover that the perfect pot that you spent hours choosing is actually the wrong one altogether.

Remember that before you select one, consider the shape of your tree as well. What shape and colors do you think are suited to the aesthetic you've chosen? Ask yourself this. Is your tree masculine or feminine? Is it better suited to a taller look or a smaller one? It may even help to keep a picture on hand so you can use it if necessary as you shop. Being able to look at your tree may help you to sort of envision the whole thing put together.

BONSAI

Chapter Summary

In this chapter, we discussed how to display your bonsai as a perfectly balanced piece of art.

- The entire display should be well-balanced, with every single aspect of it well-thought-out and intentional.

- You may want to include a companion object, but never go for more than two at a time.

- Choosing a pot for your bonsai is just as important as the tree you've chosen out. Make sure they work well together.

FINAL WORDS

The art of bonsai is a bit tough to manage, but if you can do it well, it will be one of the most fulfilling hobbies you can develop. Being able to cultivate something into a beautiful piece of living art is incredibly satisfying, and many people come to love their bonsais the way they love and care for a precious pet. Your tree is something you'll spend a significant amount of time molding and growing, and it's only natural to develop an attachment to it. The more care you give it, the healthier it will become. The more you care for it, and the more you try to balance it out, the nicer it will look. All of your efforts will show on display when you finish your plant, and the compliments you'll get when your friends and family see it will be worth the effort.

As you begin trying to grow your plant to the best of your ability, there are some important considerations. For example, you want to consider what kind of image you will create with your tree. Do you want it to be strong and firm, or do you prefer a delicate, feminine image? Do you want a tree that will be green all year round, or would you prefer to have a tree that has foliage for most of the year? Do you want something that flowers?

You'll also have to consider the various shapes that you'll put into the process. What kinds of shapes would you like to make? Would you like to create something that's flowing? Do you want something that cascades or something upright? These are all personal choices, and there's no right or wrong answer. Ultimately, in bonsai, you've got the freedom to do whatever you may want to do, even if it is unconventional. To create a bonsai is to create something reminiscent of yourself; it is to make something beautiful and as unique as you are.

Caring for your bonsai may be tough at first, but stick to it. Especially if you choose a beginner's tree, you should find that whatever you choose will be just as resilient and willing to work with you as you are to work with it. Not giving up is essential. This craft may take years for you to master, but the more you work at it, and the more you learn, the better you'll be at it. Being able to take care of your tree will become second nature to you after you've been at it long enough, and you'll hardly be able to remember the struggles you had at the beginning.

Remember, this hobby is one of mindfulness and patience. It is waiting for nature to have its way while also cultivating and guiding it into something beautiful. You're taking nature and molding it in your hands, little by little. Before you know it, it'll be ready to enjoy, and you'll be finding display stands and companion objects. You'll get compliments on such a beautiful plant. And you'll get to enjoy the satisfaction of knowing that you nurtured it into the condition that it becomes.

This ancient art is still practiced today for a reason. It's about beauty. It's about harmony with nature. It's about creating something and taming the wilderness. It's

BONSAI

about harnessing the longevity and adaptability of trees to create a beautiful image for all to behold, and if you play your cards right, it's about enjoying every moment of it.

Patience will go a long way, and you may even find that the quiet routine of it all becomes a ritual for your day. It's a moment of quiet serenity in which you get to interact with a tree and soak in its beauty. To have this is a wonderful experience, and to be able to enjoy it is one few will be able to claim. So, what are you waiting for? It's time to get out there and start growing your own!

Printed in Great Britain
by Amazon